BLACK APPLE

COLLECTED

PROSE POEMS

1975-2022

ONE BIRD BOOKS
AVAILABLE AT AMAZON.COM

Door by Mary Kane
The Ant and the Map by Judith Benét Richardson
Harlequin's Guitar: A Fable in 67 Improvisations by Jim Morgan
Little Hours: A Novel by Lil Copan
Procession of Souls by Jim Morgan

Black Apple

Collected
Prose Poems
1975-2022

Eric H. Edwards

One Bird Books • Hatchville, Mass.

Acknowledgments

@ Copyright 2022, 2023 Eric H. Edwards

3rd Edition

Most of these prose poems appeared in some form or other in PeKa Boo Press pamphlets or chapbooks; others appeared in Harlequin Ink Press chapbooks.

Black Apple would not have happened but for the affectionate though sharp encouragement of fellow travelers Judith Benét Richardson, Jim Morgan, and Mary Kane, editor of One Bird Books. But for them I would be nearly a solipsist.

Editor: Mary Kane

Layout: Jim Morgan
Cover art: Phyllis Hartley, "Apple," cast cement
Cover photo: Jim Morgan
Pen and ink drawings: Rebecca Edwards

Cover design:
Jim Morgan and Eric Edwards

ISBN: 978-1-7339200-5-6

One Bird Books
Hatchville, MA 02536
www.onebirdbooks.com
onebirdbooks@gmail.com

Contents

Black Apple
    Black Apple   2
    The Worm   3
    The Man in the Apple   4
    The Conversation   5
    The Model   6
    Malic Acid   7
    Larva   8
    Apple Head   10
    Le Cabinet Particulier   11
Crows   14
White Wash   15
Poems of Light and Dark   16
Dorothy   20
What Is Poetry?   22
Window Tappings   26
Dandelion
    Dandelion   28
    Dandelions   29
    The Dandelion   30
    Dandelion Song   31
Four Riddles   32
The Children's House
    Neighborhood Kids   36
    The Singer   37
    Musical Chair   38
    The Sunken City   39

FOUR PROSE POEMS CAUGHT AND PRESERVED, LIKE
    VICTORIAN BUTTERFLIES FOLDED INSIDE AN
    ENVELOPE
- THE PATH OF STONES   40
- COMMON ST. JOHNSWORT   41
- NEARBY IS COONAMESSETT RIVER   42
- GLASS ISLAND   43

THE SLEEPER   44
NIGHTCAR   45
BROKEN TWICE   46
ROOTING ABOUT IN VIOLENCE   47
FIVE SENSES   51
SOMETIMES X 6   53
WEEDFLOWERS
- BLUE TOADFLAX   55
- YELLOW WHORLED LOOSESTRIFE   56
- VENUS' LOOKING-GLASS   57
- RABBIT'S FOOT CLOVER   58
- HOP CLOVER   59

TWELVE NETSUKES
- MAN CARRYING THE ARM OF A DEMON   60
- YOUNG BOY   61
- MAN WITH LONG HAIR   62
- TURTLE MAN   63
- ON THE BEACH   64
- OCTOPUS   65
- BAG OF RATS   66
- WHITE MOON RABBIT   67
- WHITE MOON RABBIT II   68
- MIMOSA   69
- APPLE NETSUKE   70
- SNAIL   71

SEVEN PROSE POEMS FOR PEACE	72
SEVEN PROSE POEMS CONCERNING HUMILITY	80
SEVEN GOD PROBLEMATICS	88
WILD ASTER	92
THE IDEA FOR A PROSE POEM	93
THE GREEN MAN	94
THE FAIRY TALE	97
THE DEATH EXIT	98
SURVIVAL	99
ELEVEN MORE GOD PROBLEMATICS	100
THE BATHROOM	114
WHAT'S HAPPENIN!	115
THREE BLIND MICE	116
CAN YOU LAUGH UNDERWATER?	117
READING AT THE BOWERY POET'S CAFE	118
THE WIND'S JOURNEY	119
THREE-EYED GIRL	120
SOME PENNIES ARE ROLLERS	121
TRAINING	122
THANKS, GOD	123
GET TO IT	124
INKADOO'S WINGS	125
THE BIRTHDAY	126
TRYING TO GET EURYDICE TO ANSWER THE PHONE	127
A LETTER	128
THE RITUAL	129
AFTER ALL	130
TRUE SORROW	131
MOON DUST	132
JELLYFISH	133
GARDENING	134
THE DREAM	135

THE SPEAKING DEEP IN THE FOREST	136
CLARITY	137
MISSION	138
THE BOAT	139
THE APPRENTICE	140
MAY I SIT IN THE PALM OF YOUR HAND?	141
WET DREAMS	142
THE HALLWAY OF CLOCKS	143
BOOKS	144
IN THE DARKEST, LEAST-TRAVELED	145
PART OF THE FOREST	145
SORROW	146
CONNECTIONS	147
THE HORN OF ONE NOTE	148
HOMEMADE CLOUD CHAMBER	149
THE POND AT MACHU PICCHU	150
MOTHFALL	151
A CAT	152
VISIT FROM GOD	154
IN THIS NEXT BREATH	156

Dedicated to my wife, Rebecca, who prefers black and white. She inked the apples.

BLACK APPLE
Collected Prose Poems

If he falls asleep, little apple tears will wake him. If he is a good lover, he will need to eat. And we must eat apples if we are to come to our senses.

Black Apple

Whoever carved it, basalt of course, gave it a stem, and a leaf that floats precariously but in fine detail above the smooth curve of endless curving away. The craftsman is unknown, some Japanese name I think. I bought it in one of those consignment stores in New Hampshire, one step above panic, the middle step of pride, way down from the cellar steps of the wealthy. What does it mean to sell the thing, mean to love the thing? G.S. said get rid of nouns! But the house! The bridge! The fountain! The gate! But Brodsky! A rose is … I Get it!; by any other name … I Get it! but if you can't smell it, you Can say it. And if you can smell it, you can't, really, say it now, can you. My basalt apple, one of those grenade-type objects that fits well in the well (ok, the palm) of the hand, like a story. Does that tree have one? Is a black hole an inverted sphere? My black apple – all surface. A noun.

The Worm

I'm a snake, but I get what I deserve, a glorious transformation from apple eating. How else to name something that eats its own shape out of the world. When someone comes across me, it's as if I had altered the taste of the entire apple. They want to devour the whole world to the core without regard to the hunger of others, and finding me they feel the whole thing has been tainted. It's a matter of possession – no one wants to come across what is not their desire. All of a sudden a holy plundering tunnel in the pyramid. And we find even the virgins were not looking for us at all. Snake of the iris, snake of the wood lily, snakevine, and snake of the world, I will even slough that apple skin for the angelic wings of something truly amazing and evanescent. Oh, if you read this know that you do not know. If you have read this, you see the only true sin is not to know, which is your only blessing. Let me through, please.

The Man in the Apple

When the wind blows, the curtain moves and then the stars shine on the apples lying on the sill. Someone was rocking in my chair when I came in – the room was at night. "How did you get here?" I asked him. "Out of that apple over there," he said, pointing to a shriveled core and skin. "Thanks a lot. That was the apple I wrote by." God, was I annoyed. "Well, if you know so much, then I'll be off," he snapped, and he got up and gave me a terrific slap across the cheek with his whole hand.

I couldn't feel anything on my cheek for a day. I was holding on to the doorknob of the front door to my house, weeping and terrified. "Let me in, God dammit, this is my house!" I couldn't get this out of my head. But there wasn't anyone in there to let me in.

The Conversation

I had a conversation with an apple. I was alone in my apartment with it. Outside was a wild thunderstorm I should have been watching instead. But I am not to be wormed out of what I want. As the storm reflected on the apple's surface, I could see the thrashing of branches and leaves, the glitter of night in the core, stars and exquisite spirals that moved in a slow current. All of the apple is tidal and as sweet as walking on a beach. It's the circulation of breath that makes the surface of the apple so smooth, as smooth as sealed lips. Moistness fogs its mirror so that we forget, and take it for something to eat.

The Model

I picked five black apples and put them on the table. I also sat down and wrote you a letter, thinking there was something to salvage between us, looking up now and again at the smooth surface of the black apples. They reflected light from the ceiling bulb, and I could see into them, almost, since they absorbed the light. I know this, and looked. I wrote you five questions, one for each apple – dark and spacious questions, each one its own conundrum and collecting its own light. When I was sure you had the letter, I began eating the apples, one-a-day, fending off the "doctor." Ha, ha! He could never grow a skin over such concentration. But you now, were you sustained; nurtured? Or did their darkness and irregular placement not compose. Is it the table? I could move the pencil and paper a little this way, and the glass could be replaced with a bottle. It's been five years since I saw you, that is, without clothes on. Oh, I've seen you on the street, or more or less in public, in passing. In company. Not vulnerable. Sometimes I think I see, reflected on the black skin of the apples, that rare texture of your skin. But I eat those illusions, and I eat the fruit of those dark years. All that separation – I eat it up – just another fall ritual.

Malic Acid

What he wanted was malic acid in his mouth. Directions:
    Press one apple until it becomes a diamond.
    Drink all energy levels.
    Save juice for naturalist friend.
No wife, no children, only names, many particular names. Acid to burn away the false tongue and speak the actions of men hence. What a laugh! Bitter bright! I walk around my town looking for one place where the consciousness of malic acid was ever in evidence. Forget it.

Larva

1
A man walking among his apple trees with a cane, no not a cane because at the end is a long sharp needle like a sharpened knitting needle – the man stoops a bit, holds the point of his instrument a little above the ground like a divining rod, and indeed it twitches and the man moves slowly one way or another under his trees. Then with a sudden thrust he drives it into the ground. The earth seems to shudder, and a tiny indescribable rasping sound issues from the hole the needle leaves behind in the grass. We knew what would happen after that. The grub the old man had just pierced would bleed into the soil, making a bump we could feel as we caressed the high grass. And we would sneak over to find the bumps and mark them in secret ways. On the day that one became completely hard, it would make a sound like we were tapping on a tiny watermelon. Then we would dig out the bump, breaking the dark crusts of earth. Inside was a glassy, lustrous, green sphere, sometimes with unbelievably pure flashes of opalish iridescence deep within. These jewels we kept.

2

Once we dug up a grub in the old man's orchard before he found it. The grub was large, white from the darkness except for the eyes, which were smooth and brilliant silvery, moon-like orbs in our sudden day. It moved back and forth, like an awkward spring, as if it could not bear to be in an empty earthless space. "Pests," the old man said when we asked, explaining how the grubs ate the tenderest roots of his trees, impoverishing the great round fruits he gained a living from.

We could not afford his beautiful fruit, but he let us have all the jewels we could find. And we have worn this jewelry all our lives, lovely, depthless green-ocean gems. And that is why they are all called "pests" now. A string of pests, pest broaches, pest rings, to remind us of our farmland origins and a childhood that was as long as a summer day and as deep as the sky.

Apple Head

These apples are in my head. On a table, in a bowl. In a still life. In the gestures of my hand. In my head. Let me see into it. I go to the orchard. The sun, with its tiny seeds inside, up there providing, providing. I stand among the trees with my own tiny seeds inside. The wind gestures, apparent only in the apples. The still life. And my wife. Always my wife in this landscape. Her red hair the sunlight streaming over these apples. Her still life. Every apple in my head is red. That is not a rhyme. It is a still life, not my wife and not a rhyme. In the gestures of my hand. There are seeds inside. The bowl of the head. Full of apples.

Le Cabinet Particulier

Introduction

Mr. E. liked to travel when he was younger, and when he went out into a city in the evening, he would invariably register for a private dining room (hence, *le cabinet particulier*) either before or after attending a theater or concert performance. He made notes on these compartments, usually listing them by color. Unfortunately, no notation was ever made as to place or date, so none of them are traceable to their source. A selection of four of these cabinets are reproduced here in all their singularity.

Blue

Oh, delirious porpoise life! Night ocean! And night city beneath the arching, leaping galactic porpoise, glittering below and out of this window I have in the animal's eye. Eating here has the poignancy of great distance. I can taste the distance each different food has come. Within each bite the watchful peace of the hurricane's eye or the pause between breaths. I feel so young tonight and as though my beast were buoying me to something. Something to rend the habits and put the heart's beating in jeopardy.

Green

No windows, but wick-lamps recessed all around, and a mirror on one wall. The walls papered with a color that became paler as it rose from the floor, giving the strange effect of the room becoming lighter even though the low illumination from the lamps hardly affect the ceiling. The table is green felt and covered with a green silk. The floor a thick black-green carpet. The world here is gentle and soft and hushed. It makes me think of nature in its most pastoral mode. The first wine a chartreuse. Then a slow creeping of fear up the backbone. The alcohol is animal. An anxiety exhales from the lettuce torn to its heart so visibly. A dread, finally, of sustenance at all.

White

This room, so intense in late afternoon – the translucence bringing the plum branches out on the shoji – sooty gray the blossom – the plum scent and the branches moving, a little – what isn't white is wood, except for the small window next to the ceiling opposite – just a panel – a foot or so, slid away – to reveal the sky and once, some part of a cloud. Later at dinner, the red embers down in the cooking pit, the black varnish, alcohol as a drug rite, fish so delicate the sound of the stream still audible in its flesh. At last, the moon, looking into the high small window, saying, "Look at me. I'm cold." From so far away.

Yellow

Of all the cabinets I have been in for the last couple of years, this one was most unique and pleasing. I remember little. I was rested. The color was very pale and hinting of iridescences. I had the feeling of rainbows fanning out from the corners of my eyes, as though I breathed color. Everything was otherwise cheery, straightforward. Gold was the trim. I had a companion with me who wore yellow and was most brilliant. It was all like the mildest sun on this most bitter of midwinter evenings. Even the blood red of the steak was forgiving. So was she. I cried, and ate meat.

CROWS

We move along the path of bread. The white pieces greedily throwing away their light. Not like us, not like the dark forest. We take the light in. It is a gift. So we take the bread in. It is a gift from the boy and girl. They deliberately leave it for us, so that they might not lose their true way. If they did not feed us we would have to hunt elsewhere for the food. We would have to eat of the dead, somewhere else. These small pieces of bread, some still have the imprint of their fingertips. We accept this impression. The children move us. Later we must fly east to join some others. This is called "gathering the night." Then the children are fed behind their eyes, and the stars, always burning like crow eyes, always open, become visible. Once that is learned, no one is ever lost.

White Wash

Amazing how quickly the white loads return to be washed again. If we could only get the white out of them, they might not come back at us so fast. But it's not fair to let them stay dirty, thus obscuring their true condition. They must be purely clean each time, allowing the line person to observe them objectively. Most often, it's true, they wear out before they become something other than white. It's the once-in-a-lifetime event that one waits for, eagerly, expectantly, never disappointed even as yet another white load washes white yet again. Oh, there is a color beyond white that is worth wearing out a great number of articles for in order to experience. How many lives have been lived out, more or less entirely, at the washline, in the service of a hopeful expectation that may or may not occur? In any event, one keeps on soiling the white. And there is a joy in that too, knowing that just living may make another chance possible, messy as life is.

Poems of Light and Dark

1.
I'm walking down a busy street in an old, stony city. My shadow is not with me! I look around for it as I go. There it is! Behind me. Just like it, too. I turn back, to avoid bumping into other people. It's gone! I turn my head again. "There you are!" It doesn't speak to me. "So," I say, "first you hide, then you follow." It doesn't speak to me. People notice I am contorting myself and talking to nothing. "I'm trying to talk to my shadow," I say to them, "but it doesn't wish to speak to me." Many people begin to give me more space on the sidewalk than my natural share would suggest. Then an older man, suspicious looking, pale and thin, stops in front of me. "Would you like me to speak to your shadow for you?" he asks. "What?" "Would you like me to speak to your shadow for you!" he fairly shouts at me. "I'm not deaf. I'm not deaf!" I shout back.

2.
That's where I am, in the middle of the night, at the beginning of spring. I go out and stand between the two cars and smoke. I know it's a bad thing, but it's like freeing ghosts with your breath. One car I use mostly for work, to deliver the mail. The steering wheel is on the right. It's white. The other car is a station wagon, maroon, used more by my wife, and as a general family car. You know, ferry the children across black seas of asphalt. The pay stinks, but it's a living while we forgive each other and worry about the cars. The cars have each their own shadow. It goes with the car, this shadow, wherever the car goes. I think of all the shadows of all the cars that ever were. That's one big shadow, parts of it moving fast, some parts slow, some still. Like an enormous flock of birds hovering just beneath us, across the surface of the earth. Anyway, I am standing between the two cars. The night and the shadows of the cars have merged. Almost spring. But the snow keeps falling.

3.
We have two black and white cats. Night and Day. Night and Day. My daughter interviews me for health class. About drugs, of course. All the police and their iron-brained health allies are obsessed with drugs. They love seeing into the cancerous body that they have produced by drooling into the glassy womb of their version of history – there it is, entire and rotten, for their children to study. "Cut here," says a caring professional. "And here. Soon you will have all the bad parts cut away. What's left is good. And strong. And healthy. Somewhat mutilated perhaps. Remember the Bible. If it offends you, cut it." The cats walk around in their two colors. They regard the chickadees with a domestic hunger and a newly discovered wonder. How can an animal be so fascinating and yet have only two legs? And yet have only two spindly, hairless legs? And the birds think, how do those cats remain upright as they fall back through the fathomless air?

4.
My youngest child has a cold, so he ends up sleeping on the couch in the living room. When flies come up out of the sink, I understand how there is a crazy life that lives mostly in the dark and out of sight. Surprising, maybe, but there it is. I still have to brush my teeth. I spend most of the evening watching a movie on television about lawyers, and after that I have a moment when I think I have really wasted my free time. I could have done something better, spent some effort on ordering the mess in my study, or written letters, or made this better. But there is this crazy life, you see, that appears out of the sink drain and flies up into the light. If I miss it, I know I have missed the lesson of the day. Which is the lesson of the night. And already it is bedtime. Time for pajamas, and in the morning that Mediterranean patio, all to myself.

Dorothy

Instead of skin pattern, this man had wood grain running over his body. So we called him Woodman. The second had no pattern at all, was impervious to pain, and straight lines of moles, like rivets, ran up and down his sides, so we called him Tinman. The third had hair all over his body that stood straight out and often stuck through his clothing, so naturally we called him Scarecrow. They suffered many trials, looking for their Dorothy. The strains of a haunting harp concerto floated in the air around them as they went down the road. The road was golden at first, then tar, then concrete, then dirt, and finally just a deer track through primeval tropical pine forest. They were saddened by their lack of success, sickened by the diseases that flew in the air around them, yet ever drawn on by the harp concerto and a consistent rhythm that they sensed, as if a magnetic pulse guided them.

Soon they came to an inland ocean and stopped to make a decision. They decided to hire the wind for a search of the whole earth. The wind came to them, smiling like a Cheshire cat, and agreed to the task on the condition that they bring to it the three wise earthworms that lived under a great and ancient longleaf pine, which was out of reach of the wind, and far away. The Woodman, the Tinman, and the Scarecrow considered this request. Something shook them into awareness, and they declined the wind's offer. The wind was angry and went away.

After resting for three days the friends built a sailing raft and left the beach. They were never seen again. Occasionally, the wind will come around the house, looking to make a deal, but I only ask for news of the three friends. The wind smiles like the Big Dipper and says that they persisted in their folly and became wise. Never enlarges on this, never ceases to be amused by it. Then the wind turns up and rushes away, shaking two or three apples from my favorite tree, just to show off. But even in this the wind is clever because the apples that fall always have worms in them.

What Is Poetry?
for Jim Morgan

1.
I let it out of me as it would go, and it rolled like a sphere and went rolling down the backyard hill until it stopped far away in honeysuckle. It was very far away. The greens were richer and the details heavy. The air was like it was close to a flower that has good, unclogging perfume in it. I went, too, but I got smaller, and I could see myself there. I was very like a child. The sweet good sun rolled by, but I could not go that far. I could only watch it sink, finally, behind a wall – voluptuous as a red plum – and the earth ate it. I let it out of me as it would go. It rolled like a sphere and went rolling away into darkness.

2.

The rumor came that royalty had returned to the things of the woods. There was a murmuring amid the new leaves and in the dead leaves all over the ground and under the underbrush. People were pulling their cars off the road, getting out and listening at the edge of it. And as their eyes emptied, more of the woods came into them – and as the radios faded more of the murmuring was audible, until a sudden bird popped out of a tree and went careening up towards a bright cloud. Nothing moved. Nobody spoke. Then the bird sang from within the cloud. There was no message in it, it was just a song about the sun and oak galls and about bugs in the lichen, about a spicebush swallowtail and a vine that had oval leaves. Then it became clear that the murmuring was just an enormous number of quiet songs, lazy and humble, from everything in the woods. And when the bird dropped out of the cloud, it was changed into a silvery dart yet also transparent as rain and singing a water song.

3.
Some man came over to us while we were lying on our towels and said in an awed voice – "The rocks are beginning to sing as the tide uncovers them!" We laughed and held up our rocks.

Jim Morgan, lying on his back a few towels away from me, sat up and said to the man, – "See that little girl over there? She's been listening to the sand for an hour. It's just like a boy's choir, only so hushed, and unobtrusive." Jim has this humorous habit in speech of using big, clunky words like "unobtrusive."

4
What is poetry? It's a chanting, a deliberate magic, slow to presume, a power when the body is empty. A mental flesh, a bird climbing a ladder of open windows, coming to the roof of light and exploding into a rain of flowers. Blood is always that beautiful, the scent of dead branches in a forest, the mourning cloak of the vein fluttering out. The dark pebbles of the brook rolling on the sandy bottom are the teeth of poetry. The mouth is water. The singing goes on, moving in and out of the traffic and up the scales of heat-shimmers until the harmony is beyond sense.

Window Tappings

1.
An odd thing happened last night night while I was writing this. Someone tapped on my study window and said something I couldn't make out, so after a couple of minutes with nothing else happening, I went outside to have a cigarette and check on it. I heard a commotion around the side of the house where my window is, so I went and looked. All I saw were a few stepped-on flowers, but when I looked in my window, I could see myself writing! Wow! Some kind of time loop or something. So I tapped on the window and motioned for me to come out. Hey! we need to talk! I would also need another cigarette, but when I checked my breast pocket, nothing. I had left them in the car on the dashboard. So I went around front to get them.

2.
I went into the bathroom the other night and overheard the shampoo bottles conversing in low tones. I was going to say, "What's up guys!" but all that came out of my mouth were big bubbles. "Quick!" I shouted to my wife, "Tell the kids to go into the backyard. I've got something to show them!" They were already there, eating blades of grass that had been coated with a white, sugary moonlight. I blew some very big bubbles for them, maybe seven or eight, and each one had a different luminescent creature in it, like the ones that live in the deepest part of the … forest. They were a little

hard to see because so much moonlight had fallen by then that everything was a little syrupy, and we could hear the light tap-dancing from the branches and coating the bubbles in slow swirls. "Hey, I've got an idea!" I said. "Let me blow a really big bubble so we can all take a ride before the moon goes down!" But no one was interested in that. They all thought I should work birthday parties.

3.
My buddy TarrHo gave me a dozen eggs and told me to go home and make an omelet out of them for my family. As I cracked each shell and pushed my finger into the break, instead of a yolk there was a jellyfish inside. I cooked them up anyway. As we sat down to eat, the lights suddenly went out and the omelets started to glow. No one could bear to eat, so we held hands and sang. By the time we were done with that, the tide had come right up over the porch and was lapping at the French doors. I opened one door a little, and three drenched cats came in and started mewing for food. So they got the omelets. Later that night, you could look into the cats' eyes and see the night sky glowing like a million jellyfish.

DANDELION: FOUR PROSE POEMS

DANDELION

The root is what makes it tough, not the fakely barbed leaves or the relenting downy flowers and downier seeds nursed on the whitest milk. No neck is more likely to be broken than the neck of the dandelion when it blossoms. Nor is there a more tenacious clinging to the earth and the dark pebbles of the earth than this tentacled root like a lightning bolt driven down and grown supple, staked deep in the heart and grown simple, a kind of terrifying guarantee.

Dandelions

Come, bees, and suck. I will suck you into the center of the sun where there is no god, only a gathering of god and then a supernova radiating outwards towards the others – lilacs, forsythia, the Greek-templed it is, the Daedalion-mazed rose, the honeysuckle and other funnel flowers, and the delicately veined tunnel of the pitcher plant.

The Dandelion

The yellow buttons on your jacket remind me of dandelions – when I pick a dandelion the green cloth of the yard opens and reveals the beautiful body beneath, the body that wants to be loved, caressed and entered first and last. Such a giving to give the flower buttons and also give the body. It is only right to enter the body with one's entire body, leaving behind only what can't help but say to someone else, "Here is the dress of your beloved. You have only to unbutton it and it is yourself as someone else, come to recognize you and love you and lead you easily through this time of falling always, falling all ways into love." This is the endless ecstasy, which is why I'm taking so long, my dear, so long, and lingering over you.

Dandelion Song

Dandelion, dandelion singing in the rain, dandelion dandelion growing in the brain, what sun is this begins to shine its radiant filaments through the mind? Dandelions make the garden go to sleep and give the traveler promises to keep, and as the stars give up their hours dandelions turn them into flowers. I wandered lonely when a crowd of dandelions spoke aloud: dangerous dandelion – one shouldn't get too near – they disappear. Dandelions – they're nobody – who are you?

Four Riddles

1.
I come out of doors and down the old cement steps into the alley. High above me the sunlight is falling on the tops of buildings, blue as an eagle, unclouded by thought. I turn right at the corner and go down the street (which is on a long hill) and the sky turns out to be dark, as though it was considering. After a long wooden bridge over a chasm and a tropical waterfall, a block of meat shops with their high windows, a block of carriages, a block of poultry, and four different blocks of fascist echo, I grab a cab and head faster into the darkness. We are rats in a maze, I think, worms in mud. Have you ever seen either? No, never. It's raining, the cab pulls over to the dock and I jump out. The rain batters me on the head, and I fall to the grass, soaked and torn. What am I?

Answer: a silk handkerchief

2.

A burning green pillar without season. Three brilliant leaves alone on a tree. Late fruit on a tree with no leaves. The extraordinary textures of the barks – rough black wild cherry, chilly marble gray maple or flaking threadbare cedar. Disease often adds something to them, these trees. What is it?

Answer: the hint of smoke

3.
First there was the dismal depot, a seemingly endless pit of tin sheds, barrels, and undecipherable pieces of machines, parts to some solar system, some fantasy that just didn't make it, running down a slope that never seemed to end, whose horizon dropped away. Second, there was all that stuff set up at night and electrified, gorgeous up in the air, heart rending, moving in silence like dancers or holy dancers. It seemed then that all memory, all description, was superfluous, too abstract for the … this celestial spectacle. Is this true?

Answer: (Now that you have had some practice, we thought you'd like to figure this one out for yourself.)

4.

The last flower-weed to bloom around here is the wild aster, a plant with tiny leaves that seems to be made up entirely of flowers. After them the wasted lots really look glum until the cedar waxwings come flying into and out of the cedars and the low clouds. That is when the bittersweet, having climbed up all the trees, especially the cedars, opens its yellow doors and discloses the red orbs blaring within. Even the black jumping spider proceeding along the ridge of the shed was held by their luminosity in the late low sun. All of a sudden, a brilliant line of silver flashed behind the spider for many feet. What was it?

Answer: his lifeline

The Children's House

Neighborhood Kids

The children in my neighborhood: one time they were all born months early, another time they were born old and frail. Once there was a crop born normal, but when they all reached the age of five together, they died at once. Now someone has confused them and they're all different in age and looks and sex, but they seem to survive better. The children in my neighborhood all play in the road. No one can get through, there are so many of them, and they raise an enormous dust cloud in the hot windless summer days. Then they walk up into the trees and sit on the branches with their huge eyes open.

The Singer

I was singing at a small underground cafe one night, when I noticed a very sensitive-looking young man sitting alone at a table midway in the rest of the crowd. I began to sing at him, and soon he was pinned. First, he wrenched his coat off, then reached for the buttons at his throat, sadness rising up in him as the words left my mouth. Then he began crying, sobbing uncontrollably until there was nothing left of him except a pile of clothes on the chair and a round tear about three feet across, floating above the table. Inside the tear were children, smiling and laughing. They were in Paradise.

Musical Chair

I have a basement apartment under a child's house. Many children play in the room above my bedroom once a week, on Friday nights. They play a kind of musical chairs, but they float or fly around the chairs; I never hear any footsteps. Just the laughter, the happiness, until one of them falls or is tripped and has a nosebleed. Then I have to get up and put a pan someplace on the floor.

The Sunken City

The moon was full and white, like a streetlamp, causing shadows to fall out of the trees and a false brilliance to shine off the windows. On the other side of the barn, if one went through the hedge there, the sunken city was on the other side. Here the houses were half submerged below the sidewalks. Ladders of all descriptions led down to the doors, makeshift wooden steps to somewhere the tops of the doors showed above the level of the street. One could look down and see the yellow lights on in the rooms – hear snatches of music, overhear conversations, the rattle of dishes. There were no children down here; they were above, flying over the buildings, swooping and moving like bats. The sky over these quiet children was a deep, oceanic blue, with no stars. No stars because the children had eaten them.

Four Prose Poems Caught and Preserved, Like Victorian Butterflies Folded inside an Envelope

The Path of Stones

The stones outside my back door are talking. We walk on them all day, going to and fro, and the bottom of our lives is the top of their world. So they talk about what we press into them, and after a long time they too seem softer and a little worn away. Though that is simply the surface, the gorgeous symmetry of the appearing and disappearing life, while the highly dense interior core longs also to be broken and dissolved, to be impressed with the weight of those concerns that we so naturally put down and overlook.

Common St. Johnswort

Such misery to grow in the abandoned places! Weed thou always were and yet — the silly little yellow flowers praying for the drunken bees to notice them in the hugeness of a yellow sun! Perhaps one will forget the roses, lilies, trumpet vines and foxgloves and land, by accident or mistake of course, and drink, because…well simply because they're there and pity (or condescension) is everywhere. Here's to the short, unmentioned and common life, the flower that blesses the highway and the cars screaming by. Here's to the flower that bows incessantly to the royal wind, to the broken plant where the blood-dashed hand of a child falls in a tragedy. Here's lookin' at you, sweetheart, your ugliness, your plainness, your almost perfect disguise.

Nearby Is Coonamessett River

Always from this house it will be downhill, down to the only half-visible river draining those unfathomable game table squares, the cranberry bogs a little inland. It is as though the orderly and the serene gave way to chaos and churning mystery. The river is always like the Tao, lower than you really want to go, less shapely than you wish to seem, moving along, but tactlessly, and without discernible purpose. Your banks are so green, Coonamessett, even your gravel. I love your clear waters, your small talk, your nobly creased forehead as you approach the ocean. An approach circumspect enough to surpass any particular train of thought, the river giving every vagrant breeze serious, momentary consideration.

Glass Island

This large cloud, shaped like an island, stays between me and the moon tonight. In another world, the lilac at my left and the privet on my right a little farther off bloom at the same time. All the butterflies pupate together, feeding all day in two fragrances. The bees go mad. I would go mad in two fragrances. Then there's the sea-breeze coming down from the cloud with its sweet salt breath. I am content it is not so. I am satisfied to have the seasons move against the will. I am reconciled to that great unknowing cloud between me and the moon, that dark window where I see my mistress more fully undressed night by night, blemish by blemish, by her own reflected light. Oh, day comes through her.

The Sleeper

I like flowers a lot, so I sleep in various flowerbeds all the season long. Sometimes I sleep out, but I have a large number of beds in my yard, so I always have a place, or places, to come home to. I don't usually sleep in the winter, but I remember visiting a botanical gardens one time with a friend, in February. We got separated, and I fell asleep for a month. Never again, I vowed, only the natural way for me from now on. My girlfriend is a sex fiend, so she never has any flowers in her house. The night we met, I fell asleep at a restaurant table that had heavy Loire roses in a vase. Why I wake up at all I don't have any idea, I mean in season. I suppose one even gets tired of sleep, like anything too good to be absolutely true.

Nightcar

Suddenly the headlights find the leaves as they leap in small concerted crowds toward the car. They are like neutrons or protons or something, the way they sweep by as if the car were not there, as though the headlight was an instrument lighting up light itself as it rushed by yellow or brown or red at the boundary of sight. Also, the headlights find the lush bodies of the raccoon, chipmunk, cat, or skunk. There's an awful thud as the bodies are opened to the universal night and the leaves of light fly away from them like loosened souls or feathers. Funny how the tread of night never wears down.

Broken Twice

The apples are hidden twice tonight – under their leaves and in midnight. The mockingbird breaks off a branch of silence, but the tree remains, hiding the mockingbird twice – before him and after him. I, too, am hidden twice – in my house and under the covers, sleeping. I am letting the body renew while I slip out the window. A bulky layer of clouds hides the blue of the sky which is also hidden by nighttime.

There will not be a lot of upward travel tonight, but I can go about just above the trees or out over the water. I love to move along the shoreline, listening to the waves, their clumsy, drooping dishevelments. I marvel at this as I marvel at no other wonder. That shambling persistence, that relentlessly pedestrian meekness that crushes the rock so – makes the hardness of the rock work against itself. Prayer.

Rooting About in Violence

1.
There are those of us, in our small religious society – we know some of them ourselves – who are luminous for their distance from violence, their relative innocence and the clarity in the air they breathe around them. Of being untouched. But Ed, we are not like them, we are the other kind, the kind that always experience the violence happening to others, we terrific voltage attracters, a ground for this fierce ripping up of humanity. The screams and the boring endlessness of misery courses down our bodies and into the sewer of hell, leaving those sufferers at peace. Does the violence, I ask you my friend, leave them and leap in a questioning arc onto our heads? As if we are climbing and very close to the divine, Ed, I say to you – never look down.

2.
There are all those people, just during the short time I've been alive, driven out of their hearts, driven out of the arms of someone else, driven out of love and into death. After-death-heaven must be a convenience of tyrants and fear. You, Ed, a survivor, how odd for you to choose to be with all those people and such as me. Or not odd at all but how clean, how shapely, and of an agreeable scent it is. I must tell you, Ed, as you sit with me, how truly small I am and that sitting with me makes you small, too. And powerless. When we are sitting together chatting about movies or the business of Friends, how undemanding our corner is, almost a vacuum, a place where people walking by almost fall against us. How ridiculous we are, how unlikely to survive anything! Sitting together utterly foolish and without power, weak, spineless, open for injury – laughing sometimes like crazy people, we get such a charge out of it!

3.

I was brought to you, Ed, to your room, in the middle of your dreaming, Ed, Ed! to wake you, take your shoulder, give it a gentle shake, wake up! Except of course it was part of the dream. In stinking, enormous spillage of blood and otherwise army green and face green and smeared with sticky clots, he was there, Ed, there with us both, except I, who had never known him, just now saw all that was in him pour out because of violence. But you knew who it was, Ed, that was part of it – I was there to wake you and you were there to name him or cry through it or shake or just remember again … ah, yes, I was there to wake you up, and you were dream-remembering it for me. We both needed to see it, to share it forever because we had put down our guns and said we would not kill ourselves again.

4.
We are two of one kind – moviegoers – lovers of the shadowy images of those who love to analyze. The absurdities of war and man's tearing apart of man. The chant. The apocalypse. The breaker. All the old ones, too, the ones we grew up with that got to us like the facts of arithmetic. This is war, this is what it does, and can we really do it anymore? For you, Ed, the answer was, yes, once, and then never again. Maybe the yes was like a ticket to the movies – after all, you came back, and came back to become whole, you came out of that dark theater, wiping the salt from your hands and the gun not in your hands. Now the worst you do is pull weeds, or maybe dispose of troubling rats. And remember. For some reason we talk like equals, but I need to hold your hand, Ed. That gives me the hand I need to lean away from you and reach out blindly in the abyss, stilling the terror, reach to pull another person out.

Five Senses

1.
She ran her hands over the bark of the tree and felt the slow pulse take her hand into itself like an electric shock. Was she being pursued? Did she want this? The circle of years was open now to her embrace, as if she were the weather, the very risenness of the tree. And so, too, the tree itself opened. She glanced over at her daughter playing on a blanket in the shade. Awful summer!

2.
Everything he put in his mouth tasted like fish. At first, the terror, the disgust. He grew thin and moody. Later he felt that genetics was preparing him for the transformation, a land and water human. He who would speak to and live with the dolphins. On this optimism, he fathered twins, but they were born with wings.

3.
Maybe, at most, a few molecules of the stuff entered his nose – they were floating by on the street when he walked into them and was inhaling. At the time. What came into his mind was a lost memory of his mother, her body powder when he was two or three – sitting with her in a bedroom. At this moment. He said, "Mother," and stepped into the busy street. A pure vulnerability outwardly, yet inwardly forgiving, saving, unbreakable.

4.
Whenever she heard that particular moment of percussion, her heart stopped. A pre-cordial thump brought her back to life twice by chance. Then it was figured out in a lab, and she was brought back a third time there. There were many tears when the circumstances were explained. On the other hand, she became a well-known mystic who lived in a remote wilderness with her family. And she knew how to die already. Perfectly.

5.
His eyes saw the day as though the seasons were compressed into seconds. It was remarkable how the solidity of objects altered. It was remarkable how a dark and painful sadness rose up out of normal speed to strip the shimmering world of its drug-speedy thrill. He wanted only to go back to his own time frame and there submit gladly to the slower way. So quickly a number of years had passed. His love. Too late?

Sometimes x 6

1.
Sometimes the mockingbird doesn't sing. One wonders if this is a refreshment period, a time to gather new material, or merely a mock on silence, to ruin our expectations, the way small vases get blown off a garden table in the fall.

2.
Sometimes there are more guests on your couch than you want. You instruct two or three of them to move to the floor, and you join them there. They, of course, turn out to be the ones you knew who committed suicide. "Oh, I didn't mean you," you say guiltily, too late.

3.
Sometimes the beach is totally under water, or the moon is hidden behind clouds. These things are not imprinted in your palm, so there's good reason to regard them happily. The horseshoe crab shell you lost as a child will be replaced when the storm is over. And (when the clouds thin out) the moon will draw the blood of your body up to your shoulders, so that you'll be ready to heft its enormous burden again.

4.

Sometimes you can take the guitar out of its black case and play it like an angel. The way the guitar is held, handled, it makes me shiver. The way light curls up in its body and goes to sleep, only to be stroked awake and come out as music. And all that other time resting in that black place like it was dead.

5.

Sometimes the sorrow of the grass lies in the way of its enjoyment of the sun. One says, "Rise up! Rise up! It's warm! The sun greets us today!" But to no avail. It draws its length out horizontally like hair, and mourns. Sometimes the Earth speaks to you and says, "Don't beat on my head."

6.

Sometimes, when the leaves on the locust trees are falling constantly in a breeze at night, the shovels will come out of the shed, dancing. They are soon followed by various rakes, hoes, pitchforks, a pickaxe, even now and then a scythe, if we've borrowed one from a neighbor. But the clippers never make it. They start out on their two legs and soon lose their balance, the legs opening and going out from under them. I find them like that in the morning, handles splayed apart, under a film of oval leaves, turtle mouth agape, as though breathless and ecstatic and very dead.

Weedflowers

Blue Toadflax

This is the song of the toad as he makes his blue flax: Snap! You old field dragon, snap! Stay away from my door! I'll make my child a vest of flax for when he goes a courting-oh, for when he goes a courting he's plain as mud splashed on a window. This will make him striking. This will get him noticed! So, snap! You old field dragon, snap! Now you are small, now you are so little, now you are as insignificant as blue sky. Now you are a vest, for a toad!

Yellow Whorled Loosestrife

The book says – touched with red in the center – and I say, I am, too, heart to heart, we are alike. But this is wrong. We are absolutely divided to preserve our one identity. I picked you to identify you, and it was I who cried out and lost my name.

Venus' Looking-glass

Just a flower on a shell, as it were. Life like a shell, tucked into its square stem. I looked and saw the sky broken into its five planes – blue, blue, blue, blue, and blue – and sex where they met. I wouldn't have guessed you would need this, this weed, this minor opulence.

Rabbit's Foot Clover

I was pulling it out of my garden, slender stem with its smoky torches, the pathetic root, like so many others. So many others. I looked up and saw the world covering itself with weeds and the gardens becoming increasingly smaller, and fewer. Until there was only one garden. A garden that intense would be very special, a single wavering emerald. Not this cloudy day. Not this constant matter of choice and assertion. Not this.

Hop Clover

Issa, I miss you. You would have liked this smaller hop clover growing in such wasted soil next to the highway. You, surely, would have said something to it that I could have written down. Me, the famous scribe. Instead, all I have is this miserable plant that grows "prostrate" and your name entangled there.

Twelve Netsukes

Man Carrying the Arm of a Demon

The hand alone is huge and clutches his back, though the arm-part which rests in the man's hands is spindly, as if the demon had been severely undernourished. The man has been walking since he received the arm and you would like to ask him why, how long, when does he rest, but some intimation of danger and apartness keeps you from speaking. So you bend down again to the weeds in your garden as he passes, only now the roots have become hands gripping the earth in a desperate struggle that makes your back ache and ache.

Young Boy

You see a boy out walking the beach. Then he ages and can hardly walk, two canes and a companion who is in no hurry, picking up shells and pebbles, talking earnestly. A newspaper appears in your hands for a moment, telling of that person's death at an advanced age, which is ridiculous because there he is, only a boy of about ten or so.

Man with Long Hair

I do enjoy it. I feel sometimes so close to Botticelli's Venus, as if I knew just how she felt, how her hair felt to her as it was blown about. And in my heart this token of sensuality makes me feel shy and masculine, as if the hair spoke for me, leaving me supple and gentle, more naked and yet more clothed in an absolute and freely flowing light.

Turtle Man

My back is ornate, a mosaic to God, a measure of my invulnerability and favor. If I turn from you, you will be dazzled and shut off. Be careful of me, for although I am slow in everything, when I decide, that decision becomes a seal of armor of long lasting utility and a finished intricate design, work that I will not need to revisit.

On the Beach

She swims at night in the ocean as if she belonged there. You can hardly see her even as she walks out and stands near you, dripping, and toweling her hair. Funny how at night she is a dark mystery and during the day her beauty is so blinding it takes your thoughts far, far, out and drowns them in an ocean that looks very much like her eyes.

Octopus

In the ocean as nowhere else, like the octopus, you are in the firm grip of the water. You are in love, too. But then the octopus lives here; you don't.

Bag of Rats

She struggles along with it using both hands. It is full, fat as a full moon, and although the bag is tied all sorts of ways with a cord, the rats have eaten holes in it to come and go as they will. I see her from a distance, going towards your house.

White Moon Rabbit

As cold and still as the moon, a dark eye the dark side, looks forever at your dark side. As for the rest, who thinks of the rabbit, the moment one catches one's breath, as just reflected light. The evening begins to eat the clover.

White Moon Rabbit II

Scrubs and scrubs the stains on the moon like Lady Macbeth. Gets all white with moon-dry dust, which is lighter than earth dust. So brave to do this to that old pan, until some unseen god dips it patiently back into black ash.

Mimosa

The leaves of the mimosa close toward evening, one leaf upon another, like pairs of lovers meeting in their bedrooms. Sometimes, too, the spoons, being put away properly, embrace each other. The sun goes down, the drawer closes; again, we pull the covers over our bodies.

Apple Netsuke

Warted, mis-shaped by disease or genetic misconformation, this ivory-carved apple is beautiful and useful as a netsuke. The stem end and two leaves are carved in relief over the top, while two wormy holes have been bored through for the leather thongs. The object brings into question the very nature of home.

Snail

Something about its chemistry provides a house. Evidently without much of a mental life, it is given a one-room apartment that, as the owner grows in length of time if not in depth of wisdom or imagination, becomes a mansion of sorts in compensation, and a foot that, though not fleet nor prehensile, also serves as a sturdy door. It comes to this: the snail is slow and lives alone, unlike us social animals who barely can manage all that there is to do in this world.

Seven Prose Poems for Peace

1.
I desired, with a lot of energy, to be able to write a little poem or aphoristic paragraph full of insight into the nature of peace, utilizing all my experience as a Quaker. And my imagination, always one of my more active faculties, immediately began to forage for goodies, somewhere, I suppose, one would have to say, in the forest, or rather make that the wilderness, of my self. From another point of view, my imagination might be a Hansel, or a Gretel, or a Hansel-Gretel, where the poverty of my desire sends these imagined, rather unwilling, children out to discover what peace is, at the risk of their very existences, or co-existences. And that's a terrifying idea, even to dream. That in order to hunt for peace I must: (1) be lost, (2) be starving, (3) be imprisoned by murderously sweet entreaties, (4) (at least some part of me) be disposed of evil, not in itself an obvious act of peace I would imagine, and (5) be somehow transported from lost to not-lost-any-more and return home again, as if for the first time, but with a sixth sense that a better way is now available for anyone willing to go there.

2.

Some people write peace poetry in just the style you would expect; what they would desire, imagine or wish for. Many write about the opposite, war itself as a kind of self-destructing argument. Rather fewer write as if they were already there and were simply trying to figure out how to get everyone else there. But of course, what is peace that we should wash our hands of it so frequently, all the time protesting how peaceable we wish to be, if only the murderous other side would just cool it? And of course the vagaries of being human guarantee that peace will never be perfect or whole, that someone will hurt someone else for no good reason, or as well will cause conflict with another group for no good reason, or as well will look on lesser-advantaged people as less valuable and so more disposable for no apparent reason leading to endless justification … and it leaves one with the impression that peace has no particularly good reason for itself any more than war does. And it doesn't. You just have to choose it, like one thing over another, one flavor rather than another, and then eat what you have chosen.

3.
One of the enduring problems about the notion of peace is how little there is of it generally. Another problem is how much peace is perceived in personal, even subjective terms. Some religions say there can be no general peace until individuals find peace within themselves. Well, I was rummaging around within myself the other day, and I found this rather lovely peace-jewel in a drawer of a piece of furniture I wasn't using so much any more and so had moved to an out-of-the-way place. Let me tell you, this kind of search takes incredible patience and persistence. I don't think most people could be expected to do this, even though the result for myself anyway was most satisfying. I certainly didn't think I would ever find much of an answer, let alone an actual jewel! And once found, of course, you always know where it is, if you don't move it around all the time. In your inner self, that is. Now, if I close the door to the room this jewel is in while I'm in there, a little light seems to seep out of it, rather white, actually, like moonlight. And as a matter of fact the other night I went outside to listen to a pack of coyotes howling in our neighborhood. The way they vocalize is extraordinary, a kind of anarchic polyphony. It took me a few minutes to become aware that an almost full moon was in the clear overhead, giving away that soft light, the kind of light that creates deep shadows and seems to come into its own only in the open. In the middle of the yard, or in the field across the way. And then I understood about my Jewel of Peace.

4.

Certainly, one can understand as an adult that the feelings of peacefulness or serenity that occasionally visit us seem to be a function of our bodily chemistry, the bio-state from which our awareness springs or emerges as it were, so that awareness of peace is a kind of after-effect, like an aurora. The ions from the sun pour down upon us and charge the very air-ocean we live in, and the sight is often magnificent, or at any rate more or less transfixing. Naturally, those great oceans of energy are continually washing over our world. We rarely experience the event as a visual treat. We rarely experience anything of it at all, normally. Especially because this happens at night, when the sun is out of view entirely. It's as if the absence or obscuring of the source allows us to see some of its invisible beauty. So it happens to some of us that the experience of violence and death causes the wellspring of what makes us alive and alert to shimmer into visibility. And if we do not cry out, we do feel how sweet it is to live, and how sweet it must be for everything to be drenched in honeyed light, and to light up in utter darkness.

5.
Peace has all the loud banging colors of a little garden glimpsed in the backyard of a house in town, and all the silence of a patriotic parade inside the little boy at the end of it who can't keep up. You know? Peace just keeps stretching out in spider threads and empty paper cups rolling around in the road. I have often wondered about the indifference of the detail, yet how vivid a detail like font makes of a word. How my own bio-chemistry works makes every difference in the font of my body, and so I want to know what I am looking at when I know I am truly awake. This is tricky, like a fox casually avoiding me as we both cross a playing field late in the evening, with the light becalmed, drowsy, and hesitant, the fox having already calculated all the distances without trying, and me just trying to see the damn animal clearly so that I might describe it later, for the heavy-furred ghost of it in words might live forever, and the moment will be one of peace.

6.

Rubbing the vague white patina off a blueberry reveals a blue planet without its clouds, an ocean-orb we couldn't live on. I say "we" to be inclusive of all of us, you my audience, and you my reader, finding this fragment long after I've been anything. We are an animal on the edge of an ocean, and there are human moments when all needs are vaguely slaked and the distractions are not compelling and the taste of blueberries in an open field off a low plant among the grasses … is perfect. The late afternoon wind shakes the wild indigo bushes as if they were to become tumbleweeds, but they stay. At the beach a breeze comes off the water from the south and as it makes itself visible up the dunes, we are all watching it and feeling the moist, salty weight of a ghost of nothingness that cannot find its way out of the creation, though it tries. And we, too, should try to find our way out of this creation, though we cannot, because otherwise we are simply murderers and not in love. How the blueberry can be overwhelming and then again all of life is not enough. If we could just step out of this world a little, at times, we might learn how to love it better and hurt it less, eat it properly and be ready in an instant to have it gone, just as the wind goes over the dune, the grass becomes still, and a cloud evaporates.

for Mary Niles

7.
And there was silence for about an hour or so, and this was peace. The big dipper filled with water then spilled the water onto our faces turned up like hungry nestlings. That was peace. I would like to be able say that living things gave up oxygen and burning life in favor of silica and sunlight, but that is nonsense. All four elements co-exist, and the loss of any of them is incomprehensible. That is why we have words like "the way" and "path," "journey" and "story." With one hand holding a hand of our other self we may have some time to "get somewhere" whether we get outside or no. But what is all that except time, may I ask? It's only time, and that is where the passage goes. As though a hand dips into the water as the boat glides along; the fingers stray in the water for a moment, then are lifted out of the water again. The memory of being wet, and not chilled, is delicious. However, the operative term there is "as though," which rhymes with "row"and less with "bough" and not at all with "cough" or "enough." We have the sensation of our bodies soaring down to earth from a great height as babies and then being lifted up again light, free, and as at peace as frail ancients. None of it true in that strict sense, mostly not even explicable. But we do burn, and much of our creating has to do with making entities that take in fuel and transform it into something else, something human-oriented. Oh, what amazingly wonderful guilt! We discover eating and all hell breaks loose! Taste! So evanescent in the mouth, keeps us interested in life. Keeps us burning. And peace is one kind of this fire, sacrificial understanding that life eats life to be alive. It's not a vegetable versus meat thing at

all. That's just a matter of taste. No, it's whether you love to be alive or you feel guilty about being alive. Those who love are at peace, those guilty can never be. So, here, have an apple and let us talk further about this, together …

Seven Prose Poems Concerning Humility

1.
This is going to be a hard thing. I sit here in silence, knowing it will be mostly silent, trying to do nothing when I know already that nothing is what happens mostly anyway. I don't have to try that, I have to try to not-do something. Anything. I feel I am in a little boat, rocking on words. Trying not to row … oops. Anyway. It's a beautiful room, really, dark vertical wainscoting, ivory painted walls, large generous windows, many-paned, as if natural light would make all the difference. Would, that is, instruct my soul into my true condition. Would, that is, make worship itself a beautiful room. The outer light touches all of me that appears, and bathes the clothes I have chosen, or rather shows up or off texts and folds, lines of stitching that dance in and out of view like porpoises. To see handiwork in natural light can be (at the best of times) lovely and true. Same is true of behavior and words. The fish-scale flash of words dipping in and out of daylight. Jellyfish purling and pulsing. A world moving slowly over stone. Or seaweed shifting here and back, anchored in darkness. I know my body is dirt, unlit dirt. At the bottom of a world. I have to ask myself what I am imagining, what becomes because of me? What have I embraced and welcomed into a revealing daylight from within? On what ground does this world become bright and visible.

2.

The phrase God is within is the core of the Universe, say the mystics. Say the Quakers. I am one of those last. Some people just can't step aside from the word God long enough to experience God, God as golden apple, as silver pear, as possession. Instead, they think about God. It is, however, easier to say God after the fact, rather than prior to. I can be trusted that far. Afterwards, we are all in a good condition, relatively. Beforehand, let's say little or nothing, positive or negative. God isn't an idea anyway, and God can't belong to us either, be a slave or a habit.

More like a companion, an x-ray, the one who sees well through, speaking me in my dark body-bag of marsh dirt. God is like pure-light-in-pure-darkness. I can't see either purity, but where pure unending darkness seems a natural, possible condition of the world from my mortal perspective, pure light seems to be an unwarranted gift, a disturbingly effortless talent, a grace without practice, discipline, or will, a being-washed sensation. The most solid rock in the presence of pure light is just an emptiness waiting to be visited and broken out of. Like my heart.

3.
The word humility, raised up so high in religious literature, is otherwise entirely negative in the world. A false morning of calm water in the strait. No one trusts or likes a humble person. Anyone behaving humbly is immediately rung up as a hypocrite and looking for some reward (like status or reputation) or payoff elsewhere (always the reward across a gulf). She is there, somewhere, alone on the beach perhaps, waving over and against the current. But the humble offer no excuses, are not sorry for anything. They see the condition of others, but they are unwilling to give the rotten fact too much weight, or to make too much of their own low condition. This curiosity of human personality, being low and at peace like a cranberry bog, enrages the passion of others. It is as if a humble person causes endless trouble with their searchingly plain news and threateningly peaceful presence. How dare you! It's unforgivable! You are not one of us! The taste of blood is in the mouth of the crowd, requiring the humble person to suffer. Suffer a lot and for a long time. Suffer for everyone who already has a job, is getting along following the rules, going to vigils, saving for retirement and feeling just fine thank you not at all for making them feel inadequate. For attacking their self-esteem. Even though the humble person is saying, "You'll do! You'll do!" And the rest are thinking, "Anything but that."

4.

Although it's a lovely and energetic result of a certain kind of work, humility has no value. The humble person is a lily-of-the-field, will be treated with literary appreciation and dismissed, or built on. There are just too many fields and bogs and all of them with their repetitious flowers spiders turtles birds and bareness, and most of the space is needed for housing for the homeless anyway. Or a place to treat effluent, or a golfing lawn. You get it. When the body has accepted the seed, the fruit thereof appears in the hands of the humble. Appears in the hands in order to be given away so that the hands might be empty yet again and ever. This is an insult to good working folk who know the value of a thing. The humble, who may have sacrificed their lives to bear this fruit, refuse to be paid. That is without a doubt the most disturbing part of their whole thing. It's so unrealistic. I mean, in the face of achieving greatness, of justly winning a great honor, of any kind of largeness at all, a certain humility is in order, for sure. It's balance. It shows us equality. But honestly, only the truly great or greatly talented have any right or obligation (if you must) to humility. The rest is just a sham.

5.
When humility grows up within someone, they are already depending towards the source of their life. This is like a flower that looks down at the ground no matter what branch it finds itself on. Or it is the wood lily, freckled and flamey, obscured in a field of high brown grasses, looking only up where there is yet only emptiness and an illusory blue (but what a blue!) sky. The humble person knows the invincibility of death and the grace of the saturating light that has removed the stain of death from their coveralls. Death neither wet nor dry, neither dark nor light, neither up or down. The stitching on these pants is for heavy wear, and the light falls on them restlessly, like lapping waves or bits of mica in a piece of pink granite. So we can all keep on breeding, and at the same time we can all keep on making the choices that others will not make. So all is forgiven, all is forgotten although not for nothing do the humble work this gentleness into a hard soil. Some things are so far off there really isn't any particular point or connection, a kite that has broken its string, and our vision as we grow older either grows fond of what is closely alive or looks off into a graceful vacancy. Even while holding onto the hand of the beloved. Humility is not indifferent, but like a looking-glass flower, its root is invisible in a mysterious dirt.

6.

I shouldn't even say this word (*water*); and then, maybe it would be better for everyone if I didn't talk about humility at all, since it upsets everyone so. Maybe that's why the word *water* is so useful, since no one these days actually, solidly, associates it with humility, or with any other virtue or characteristic. I say *water*, and everyone knows right away it has run out of my hands more quickly than ink from this pen, and no words form at all. Empty of mind. Everyone more or less accepts water for what it is – mercurial, opaque to understanding, uncertain in its transparency, at times valuable for consuming, like air. Good for Nature, rah rah, all that in the correct amounts. But then, even Nature doesn't know how to handle water. But even then a lot of people think that what all the dry places of the world need is a little more water. They would condemn to death everything that thrives in desert. And that is so true of right here and now. We live in a swamp. If we lived in a desert we would value water too much and fight over that. That our bossy bodies would be squeezed by everything around us. Better we live like our ancient parents, the slime algae of the oceans, where water is taken as obvious, or overlooked entirely. Like the perfect blue air. We could be a modest species, in fact, in marsh and desert, and simply be overlooking the fact because we are always staring up and out at an empty, dry, blue sky, imagining a rain-cloud.

7.
I am back in the silence. It is better this way. I have discovered that wherever and whenever I stop, God might begin. This is my Big Bang theory of humility. The universe is the size of a point and at the same time it is as big as it is now. And getting bigger every day. I'm not. I am full size, done with the growing body, going on to … I don't know. I know that I started to go away from God, at some point, and then I turned around and started back. Or is it the other way around, like a breath. Taking God in and then letting God go. This is actually pretty funny, but no one is sitting around here breathing hard and laughing. Everyone seems to be terrified and/or trying to think of something. I think we should be terrified to meet God and we should be aware that God does not appear in thought. There is nothing to think of, nothing to be afraid of. Of course, there's a problem there. Here. If we could meet God the same way we meet other people or situations, yes, that would be terrifying. But that wouldn't be God and that doesn't happen. God isn't exactly out there. God is absent everywhere we look. God is absent even within ourselves. God is at the center of creation, the big bang, and creation has no center. It began. Alpha. There is its center. We began. That is the center. God is where we began. We are there and we are not there. God comes to us. Always. Big Bang. Reaching out, always in the center. Drawing us down with gravity, the weight of dirt, moving over stone, expanding into nothing, which is the same as love, forgiveness, gentleness. The beginning, now. Right now. No, sorry, all that meretricious now language. Like a sink full of dirty dishes. I mean the Very

Beginning in this moment. That's it. That's all. The end. Hard though. A hard and humble thing.

Seven God Problematics

1.
God had had his day and men were tired of it. God gave the day to women, but they didn't want any part of it, given the past and all that. God offered it to dogs, no one knows whether in spite, exasperation, or simply the ongoing alexandrine thread of generosity that seems to run around the universe accompanying God in an entangling meander of instantaneity. Dogs accepted it with an immediate servile appreciation they could not get out of their genes, apparently. People were quick to take advantage.

2.
The back of God hosted the great deserts, the great oceans, but not the great mountains that reminded folks of the other side of God they were afraid of. Actually his back was not all that smooth up close, cluttered with underlying structures welling up from within, dubiously scientific, and surface anomalies that resembled cherry angiomas, polyps, warts, and moles. Occasionally, God would want to scratch something back there. The quandary set up a terrible and energetic moral storm somewhere in the impenetrable forests at the edge of God's back.

3.
God gave some people some sharpened sticks. Of course, all faithful readers will know at least potentially where this is leading. The sticks were used wisely or unwisely, cruelly or benignly. Some were injured, others

died and more were left unaware. A theology of doubleness arose, left foot right foot, hands, sense organs, male and female (Plato, old style), heaven, hell, belly buttons, a seemingly endless clarity or intelligence of purpose or at least design. In between all this doubling sat a space, a connecting place. You could take a stick and pry away in it until whoever it was gave up whatever secrets they had held precious but now seemed meaningless, or they died.

4.
A white cup is on a table. The cup is ceramic, the table wood. So far this description idles like a car with an oil leak. Moving right along … the cup is very Zen. Its no-smell has the stench of Zen flatulence; the lack of anyone in the room, like a "teacher," also smells of sweaty Zen, of Zen absence. The table, however, does have a faint aroma; wax or cleaner or residual barf from last night's drinking session. Hard to say, and who wants to say, anyway? I don't. Now where did I put that hammer? No, not to smash anything like the cup or the table, but to kill the person I was drinking with last night. God's absence and Zen presence are really helpful here. Or not.

5.
The car in front of me swerved violently before it went off the road, crossed the breakdown lane (I thought that fact was singularly diagnostic), and ended up in my rear-view mirror in a ditch. I called it in by opening my window and howling like a dog. I told the story later on to some friends, one of whom it turns out had been in that car. Life is so basically complex. Rudderless, causeless, pointless, full of detail like pollen. I did become sick, maybe from the anxiety. Other people's actions, sometimes from a long distance away, can change a person. Their direction.

6.
God was sitting outside at a cafe having a drink (tea maybe). Things were not going well for some of the people around (him?). They fell down and broke their arms, or something on their faces. Blood everywhere. God was thinking (who would have thought that?) how on earth did I get here? Where am I headed? And how do I get out of this? The police said they would process (him?) like everyone else. God hated that suggestion. The policemen fell down dead.

7.
When I first came to God nothing out of the ordinary happened except that normally I would still have been asleep, except for the person I was sleeping with woke me up saying, "It's nearing time for meeting. Get some duds on." I did it but with misgivings. Misgivings are old French fries one keeps from yesterday's fast food, thinking, "I can heat these up tomorrow and they will be great." Of course, nothing could be further from the truth, except maybe Catholicism. So anyway, not being Catholic even if I am catholic, I went along easily enough, considering, as I went, what Kafka might have thought staring at the back end of the person taking me to a room full of comfortable, gray upholstered chairs with arms. "Embrace me," I said to myself and hoped for the best, or at least nothing at all, which is where I discovered, later on, God hangs out most of the time.

Wild Aster

In November, all that is left of the wild asters is this kind. The others are dead and make up the brown withering fog that lines the roadsides. But this aster is a little shorter and less visible, and still green. Its leaves are more like needles and its flowers are tiny. Maybe because the weather is cold the flowers seem barely to open at all. They are minute buttons, open at the top with some white petals sticking out like short threads. In the very center of these brief white petals is the feminine heart, sun, a golden inwardness and warmth that succeeds, where I can see my breath, to make my imagination fertile. What, I have to ask, is attracted by this? What tenuous scent pours out of it that I cannot feel? Perhaps nothing but the wind because most of the insects are dead, except for some strange flies that sit on the tops of mailboxes even now if the sun is right. Lots of plants use the wind, few such a cold one. The end of a season, where we are looking to go indoors. Even so, the wild aster keeps up its life and extreme dedication. So do the monks to my othering lifestyle. And for all artists suffering to create only the most wonderful of experiences, here is the wild aster, an aster like a patron saint, not even worth picking to bring inside for a few days of joyous if humble contemplation. Worth only leaving alone. There are incredible flowers at the extreme edges of our capabilities, and we could know them, regardless of how plain they have to be. Regardless.

The Idea for a Prose Poem

Recently, the idea for a prose poem came to me in the dead of the night. Either this is a good time for what some may refer to as inspiration or it's the worst. Someone in a back row scoffed when I said that the other day. "It means dead-center, not deadness," I replied. Fool. This moron obviously never read Jonah when he was awake. Either way, it doesn't really work I had already realized because in the dead center of anything, like a tree for example, it's still dead we're talking about, and dead anywhere is either a good place for an idea or a dismal one. If you have discovered the red-centered and scented wood of the cedar, that's a scent you might die with happily enough, but if you find that ants have hollowed out for its entire height the core of a great oak, standing otherwise proudly in the middle of your yard, that's a crawling dead-center of an entirely different sort. Like grace itself, it occurred to me later: either you experience it or you don't. There are no helpful explanations for that without the experience or its inkling. Some say you have to do exactly the right thing (or things) to have this bestowed upon you, and some say there is nothing at all you can do. Now this idea for a prose poem came to me, and it wasn't a pleasant one, so I'm not going to burden you with it, at least not right now. But the fact that it came to me in the dead – really out of the dead – of the night was consoling in its difficult way. That I had nothing in the dead of the night and then I had something. That was appealing.

The Green Man

Here in the backwoods there is a certain moldy smell of dirt and roots. Leaves disappear from the forest floor. He knows all manner of things die out here, alone, away, under the trees, in any sort of weather. Not exactly a solution to anything, just a certain organizational breaking down and getting reorganized. Appalling as that is, a bit abstract except for the hinting smell. The smell is talking now, to him, as he stands in what looks like the path, but no one is coming by any time soon. As he wishes. He himself is lost. More or less. It's an easy plan to execute here. In the city he would've had to hide. Some number of well-meaning good-ish Samaritans of undisclosed religious affiliation would have made sure to have him looked at, picked up, IV'd, interrogated with care, maybe even love. Every city has a hospital. Hospitals are the opposite kind of vulnerability. Only in the woods, and preferably in a forest, are the warnings of caring even loving folks are given professionally, pointedly, in advance, to ward off just what he wants. And that is to be open and vulnerable to the forest itself. To embody with his whole personality the willingness to be part of the forest again. How long ago was it? Also, he used to dream he was a Green Man. Certain limitations, but a definite set of qualities he admired, wished to possess, not simply profess. That was a phrase of his religion, not to profess what one does not possess. Or at least desire to possess in this modern age of carefully misplaced speaking, another advice of his religious affiliation. About plain speaking. Well, in some sense then, if not of God, at least his own love of nature, of the non-human natural world. Of course, nothing deliberately comes out to die here. Nothing he's ever seen simply wandered away into the woods with the express intention to die. His neighbor told him once, the one who keeps chickens, those endlessly murmuring leaf-kicking birds, that after a few years he stopped taking his non-layers to the local co-op farm where some of the workers would use them for food. Instead he took them into the woods and let them go. They probably lasted a day or so, he said, before some predator happened upon them. After all, they aren't truly wild. Or all that fierce. They just get a few days of freedom. Whatever that means to a chicken, he thought. Aren't chickens more or less social? A pecking order? Not to be confused with sociable. He wasn't sociable. He didn't think chickens were either. He liked chickens. Some of them had the most beautiful feathers to boot. He had wanted to be a Green Man, not to die but the opposite. He was confused. He felt uncertainty in his desire. He felt uncertain and uneasy. In the pathless woods looking for a kind of immortality. Regenerative. You could cut off his head and he would pick it up and go away, go even deeper into the forest. Not running around like a chicken with its head cut off. What the Green Man wanted was something else. To be disenchanted, to be free of cruelty and the cruel logic of fables. To show a person something great that would change the way people lived. Liberate them, preferably in large numbers. Overwhelming numbers. The Green Man, who wants to die but can't, and the man who wants to live endlessly but can't, and in the middle a chicken with one or two days. As the sun goes down, our man, standing amid the trees somewhere in a forest, becomes harder and harder to make out.

The Fairy Tale

I wanted to write a prose poem where the mysterious place between the word 'prose' and the word 'poem' became alive and thrilling. Actually, besides 'alive' and 'thrilling' a lot of other words did come tumbling out of that empty in-between-space, words like 'astounding' and 'feral' and 'moving,' words that evaluated what I had not yet imagined or acted upon except to start this, words of energy and hope. I know I would have preferred creatures with uncharted lives to be born out of that gap-that-ensures-meaning, lives like a Rumplestiltskin or Hansel and Gretel's witch, or even a blue fairy or a goat, for God's sake. A gruff one. That would have given me a story. I could have said (written) the story and you would have the story for yourself, like an inexpensive but deep though small original work of art. "That creature's story lived for me," you could say, and every time you crossed the street to the more-than-tree-shaded sidewalk across from your house, you would think there was a bit of the power of fairytale in simply walking into town. Even just to buy a loaf of bread.

The Death Exit
(for H. Richard Niebuhr)

I have to tell you, both of us being on the other side of this thing, death is not an exit. It's a stop. A door that, if or when you die, you open for others. To be clear, it's your door and no one else's, but you open it, even as you don't go through it. That would be life with others after you die, and while I can gently if without absolute certainty assert that you won't have that (I don't), I also am here to say you don't exit anywhere. You stop. Stop breathing, talking, associating – living in short – but you don't exit from life. Others now pass through the door you have opened for them, which is perfectly their lives after your life. Some of them will be aware of this life long after you've stopped. Some of them will rapidly tire of what I call "The Doorman Syndrome," and prefer to nap. I call it napping, but then, I could call it anything couldn't I. You wouldn't know the difference. It doesn't matter. What I want you to know is that your death is not an exit for you; it's an exit for everyone else.

Survival

Living on is the easiest thing. Coming to the end of meaning is a bit harder, but we are advised to cut down field of vision and depth of field. "A little myopia is a fine opiate" is a famous phrasing of it. The wind blows the dead leaves over the green grasses, and there is nothing to do but walk on, whether with or against the wind. With it is easier, following those leaves. Against it is no better and the air makes the eyes tear. Why are you running upstream, little fish? Oh, very little fish, sometimes with a great hate, rarely with love, mostly with embarrassment and the fifth sense of inadequacy. Look at you at the edge of the lawn. Can't you feel even the slightest expectation as the universe plunges over another moment? And I mean, this universe awaits your decision each instant so that it might flow as it must and not have to rescue you like a lover racing by on a horse to lift you up, take you away from all of this.

Eleven More God Problematics

A.
If you are completely honest tell me, as I am attempting to be every day, not even knowing what would constitute that virtue in its completeness. I take a breath, a ragged, rugged, rule-breaking ridiculous but revelatory breath, and in all my dishonesty I know that breathing is both completely honest and murderous. What worse can a person do than murder? Is there such a thing as an honest murder? Even to hurt another inadvertently leaves an indelible mark, but the other, I shudder. Shuddering is honest enough. How to parse honesty from injury. Take two examples from the portion of the Bible that is strictly if not entirely honestly devoted to the Christian movement: Lazarus and Judas, brothers in a story where they have lost all agency. Whatever they might have claimed for themselves, they cannot remove the chains they were imprisoned with. I am speaking, of course, about the words, the so-called Gospels, in which they are fixed like flies in amber, visible, still, perfect yet only giving of themselves what the words will allow. They are porcelain vases into which the tears of the world collect and stiffen in their small hollows. God had to come along, just today as a matter of fact, as every day, to free up these poor men, break their chains and liberate them. How does God do this? By making their stories dishonest, unreal, and never allowing the words to escape the page. Can you honestly claim that Lazarus comes back from death, like a quick stop at the local convenience store for a lottery ticket? Gone and back.

"Hey guys, check it out, I WON!" Horrifying. And Judas. No one names their kid Judas. Nice work, words. And tell me reader, honestly, was there anything more completely, more utterly honest than that kiss?

B.
God was touring. Giving lectures to various groups, gender specific (or not) depending on the audience. Sometimes, most irritating, as God ground teeth placed appropriately, God would like to have pointed out that God was not a reproductive entity. Gender irrelevance was a point God wished not to have to make every time God spoke. "What's so freaking unclear about I am that I am. Jesus! People! If I didn't love them I would surely …," but the thought was washed away into an indefinite but more or less causally certain future. As Peter drove God from one venue to another, God idly considered black holes, wondering if they were just a projection of God's darker emotional moments. "Think Positive" also ran through God's mind, like a rabbit attempting to avoid a predator, real or assumed. Both actually. Reality per se didn't constrain God particularly, but it did occur to God how everything good seemed doomed to extinction sooner than later. Sigh. The worst, though, were the endlessly long car rides. Cars were a particular favorite thing of God. No company. Peter reliable as, well, a decent navigator and general secretary. Up front, ready to go. God appreciated that. There was no master-slave thing going on between them either. Peter is The Man, God thought. Quiet. The length of the trip, rather than simply appearing here, appearing there, wouldn't have bothered God all that much, given the temporal constraints, except for one thing: Peter was constantly being stopped by the police. Driving while Black. This stopping, explaining (sort of), being pulled over then pulling back onto the way, the road, whatever, yet again, as if starting over and over. This thought, a piercing

black hole in God's mind, made God think perhaps it was, after all, maybe no one's fault. No one's fault. No one's fault. Just holes in the universe into which something disappeared and something else arose. It's just me. All me.

C.

There was a time when God was just God. Something rose to the surface, was given a name, and moved on. There was a time when Peter was driving around before cars, before chance, only trees and rocks and weather and lots of animals or almost-animals of all sizes. Peter was driving a spiffy (if he did say so himself) new hybrid, and it felt to him anyway like the world was taking a turn for the better. God was just being God, genderless or not, embodied or ghostly, present or not. All the same to God. Even existing or not. All the same to God. Peter, on the other hand, thought this was hilarious, people calling it spiritual, for God's sake. Sometimes with a capital S, for God's sake. As if! He would turn around in the driver's seat, keeping his hands on the wheel, of course, and smile at God, who would wince back at him. God knew what he thought. Peter loved that about God. They had a great time together.

D.
God wanted to be welts and hives on people, and animal skin in general. For hundreds, maybe thousands, of years, welts and hives of all kinds came and went. Practically an infinite variety just in the welts and hives department. God loved it all. Some were covered, some barely touched. God kept a hand, or a paw, or intention in every bit of it. All of it. People wondered where God was. But God was all over them and in them, loving the feeling, the sensitivity. I don't know how to satisfy this particular itch, God thought, since this wasn't an experiment or a test or anything except presence. One had to steer clear of obsessiveness, perhaps. The way opened then in God's mind for moles, and other anomalies, even as God remembered that presence worked just as well in a pain-free environment. Or did it. What about the metaphorical itches and dis-colorations that plagued or blessed people, and the potential to combine both disease and inspiration with these specific moments? Job, for example. And this was just the tip of the proverbial iceberg, or thistle, or whatever stings.

E.
God decided to be like a person for awhile, thinking androgyny would be a good strategy so people could take him/her/it as him/her/it and be happy. Everybody happy. What a concept. God liked it. This person-like God gave a poetry reading. God had in fact sworn off writing for what seemed like either a long time or an instant, and felt it would be interesting to see if words worked out any better with all the new technologies and methodologies around. And so many folks could actually read nowadays, one way or another, what with all the new technologies and methodologies around. The reading went well. The room was upstairs in an old fire hall, small but crowded, a good-size crowd, God figured, considering it was summer, and people had choices on how to spend their evenings, at least here in good old wherever this was. Maybe on to bigger venues? However, directly after God had finished the few new poems that might occur to an omniscient, omnipresent being, albeit for the moment in almost perfect human form, people surrounded him/her/it with requests for copies. Was the book out yet? When? What was the lucky publishing house? They wanted the texts. They were afraid they might not remember them perfectly. Some clearly hinted they had tried to memorize everything they had heard. A few, hanging in the back, were already arguing over whether God had said Yea or Nay in one or another of the poems. It was distressing. This is why Peter, God's driver and closest friend who had taken him to dinner beforehand, modeling the standard format for visiting poets, and was doing all the driving as long as God wished, found God around back of the building

down near the water, burning the poems. "Let's go," said Peter. "It's a circus in there. Let's skip the cookies. They've actually divided themselves into groups to try to remember what you said and write it down first. It's a mess. All argument and regret for not paying enough attention. I think they expected you would be announcing the publication of a new book. At least now nothing can be taken for granted from you; plus, if they saw what you're doing right now, they would go crazy. It isn't safe being anywhere near here." "Big mistake," God said absent-absentmindedly. "I haven't dealt with either infinity or nothingness well at all, have I. I shouldn't be out in public; that seems obvious." And that's how that evening went.

F.
God took a walk on the beach. This is what people do at this sort of place, right? God's steps left no imprint on the sand. God thought, maybe they should be immutable, unchangeable by the sea, impervious to weather. My creation, God thought, I am in it but not of it. I can enjoy it, but it's such a small part of the whole thing, these steps. My creation, what I like to think of as my work, has left no mark of my presence or absence, not now, not then, not to come. God thought through to the omega moment, which of course was as present to God as anything else. Good grief.

G.

God hadn't been present for some time, but not exactly absent either. The word that came to God was *lurking*. Just around the corner. Maybe next year. At the end of time certainly, but perhaps sooner, glorious return. Fit for a King. But if God hadn't exactly been gone, then what? God enjoyed lurking. God had discovered something God could enjoy without feeling infinitely bad all day for doing or not doing. An infinite in-betweenness. Not this. Not that. Not even a freaking paradox! Just Lurking. Sign in shop window (or door): JUST LURKING. The word was magical. It had the feeling of dark clouds, heavy organ chords, and small lights at some distance at night. Far out. I am so close to everything, God thought, and lurked off without moving.

H.

God had come to dislike plans, and didn't plan to make any, in the same way all things had to be considered and played out for God, in no particular order because order is a temporal construct. A young man prayed to God, "How do I die happy? I want to die knowing, feeling the presence of, possessing the physical substance of – happiness. I find the difficulty even of possessing this desire to be insurmountable, so I am unhappy and appeal to you, your loving nature, to explain, disclose, or dispense a positive answer. I can suffer much if I can die happy." There was silence in the heavens for a remarkably genuine amount of time. The young man was patient, being temporal. "Join the Club," replied God. "But there is no Club."

I.

God made a mistake. There was no doubting the fact, or, once having committed the "error," much like any other act God had done concerning matters of fact, an indefinite number of them spread out across the universe in a thin film. Then God reflected upon this mistake as one might gaze at something, though less clearly through a fine screen, and realized not only did God have to make this mistake if God is truly God, but that every conceivable and inconceivable mistake might possibly be necessary if God is truly God. If I am who I am, or rather that I am, no mistake is so great that that mistake cannot be taken as a sign. Not consoling but consoling nonetheless. Not a happy logic, but then what logic is? I make mistakes, thought God, although up to this point God had only made the one. A left turn that should have been a right. The wrong spoon. The wrong men. God pulled over and stopped (God had in fact been driving unaccompanied, uncharacteristically). Peter should be driving, God thought. Mistake, or lesson learned? The difference? This is crazy! God knew this even as he thought it. Do I have to do crazy, too? And he knew the answer to this even as he thought it.

J.
Peter was driving, God in the back as usual. Peter loved this car, or whatever it was. GPS, beautiful big screen mounted next to a lovely, deep-set dashboard display. Several of the options seemed obscure, and indeed, most of them were not highlighted and so unaccessible, God not having subscribed to any of them. Especially if they cost additional money. Which, of course, they did, neither police nor deity receiving freebies any more, at least that anyone might trace. Ah, the untraceable, thought God. How like prayer. Or some particles God preferred to keep out of measure, at least for the time being. Just then Peter drove off a dock that the GPS had assured him, in her most calm and reassuring tone, was the arrival at their destination. As the car sank into a green marble-like and liquid light, God rolled down the window. Of course, no water came in, giving God a sentimental or perhaps vaguely pleasant if guilty nostalgic memory, if God experienced such things, which of course God did. Does. Peter damned the GPS, slid the car into all-wheel drive, and continued to drive. "Not impossible at all. Give me maps any day," Peter muttered, "instead of this effing fake and not wholly reliable navigator. Not even real!" "So!" God's voice interrupted the stillness of no wind passing by the windows, "Can we not do the unreal just as much as the real? I get tired of facts 24/7. Let's get some fiction on this bus and give ourselves a break, or a holiday, or whatever we want to call it. Let's live it up a little!" So they did that in some dimension or another, accountable to no one and nothing for at least one version of all time.

K.

God was meta. This was not where God wanted to be, ever. Necessary maybe, but God preferred the simple and the direct most of the time. Or times. However, there it is, God thought, now and again I have to go there. God save me. This was a little private joke of God's, best when Peter was driving because he simply hated that joke. "Lighten up," God always said to Peter. Then they would both laugh. So meta. The problem, to put it in overly simplistic terms, was infinity. Not infinity per se, not the infinity of mathematicians or even philosophers (God love 'em!). Rather the infinity of infinities within every infinity. This was God's house without a doubt. I would rather be on the road than cleaning out a bunch of foggy demons yet again from my otherwise pleasant and well-deserved country place. But it had to be done now and again, so God was meta. No roads there, no high German Romanticism trekking the woodland trails. No Let's Wander! It was almost work. You see, for every infinity that went on forever, there was an infinity of infinities off that, and so on. It was the closest God ever came to considering the non-entity entity that had the name God. No way to begin an infinity (Zeno, you shit), no end once begun. Paradox unresolved was the only respite in such a place. And besides mastering nothingness, God knew that the only thing to do in this endeavor was simply to stop and wait. Simple. It made God smile. Nothing like happy, but close enough for all practical purposes.

The Bathroom

You see, you have a roll of toilet paper that sits on top of the heater cover against the wall, to the right and a bit in front of the toilet itself. Easy to reach. Directly to the right, actually crowded into the corner between the toilet and the heater, is a sink. No ordinary sink, even though it looks ordinary, at least, as ordinary as you might picture it without having been there. No, the water that comes out of the faucet when you go to wash your hands, at last, having done everything leading up to this moment, the water that comes out is marvelously fragrant, like lilacs or freesia or certain daffodils that are more delicately scented. The temperature is always perfect. No adjustment is felt, by the hands, to be needed. There are no pipes leading to the faucet. You can check the cabinet underneath by moving a small wooden latch to one side and look around. There is the drain for the sink, as for the toilet, going through the floor, but no pipes bringing water in. This being completely nonsensical, physically impossible, makes you straighten up, turn around, regarding two doors at right angles, both closed. One returns you to wakefulness and youth, the other to a bedroom where you lie dying, breathing and tasting the stale weary skin of your mouth. Why leave? Why stay? The people you love have died or departed, some unwillingly. You take some water from the faucet in your hands to sip, hoping it will cure you of something, or at least mask the necessary business of making choices. Of gaping.

What's Happenin!

It's hard to stop. Once begun, one might as well go along with the flow of time, whether we feel old or that we haven't changed, not really, not essentially. Or whatever. The arguments about change are stupid anyway; the flow of time is something else again. Kantish. Nothing needs to happen as time goes by. The daffodil does not need to fail before my eyes, before the regard I offer it of myself, not just my eyes. The child waiting for the bus at the end of the dead-end road tells me when I ask, "Nothing. I'm waiting for the bus!" Time flows: nothing happens. I sit here waiting for God. Most of the time, to speak precisely, nothing happens. Time flows! Nothing has to happen, though much does. And as it chances, the more time that occurs, so to speak, the more it's possible that something happened along the way, might happen at some later time, and is perhaps happening now, even as we wait. I find it hard to stop, but on the other hand, I like to.

Three Blind Mice

The professor was making his final statement before being hauled up the steps of the gallows. He said, "I live non-fiction 24/7, so I prefer to read fiction when I read." I had heard this before; actually all of us present, meaning myself and the three blind mice who had signed up for his class, a "hyper-graduate workshop" so-called, that he taught entirely by semaphore, us on one hill, the prof on another. For the mice, well, they guessed, surmised, speculated, basically mostly waited for me to write or prick actually what he said, in braille. I guess they spent most of their time up there listening to (or feeling the effect of) the sighing of the pines, which they couldn't see moving in the winds. They danced occasionally, but they were not the dance. What we were about to witness would be the dance. The gallows was rickety and thrown together overnight out of pallet wood, jammed up with what the carpenter called "wires" instead of nails, that he shot from a pressurized gun. There had already been a number of admissions to the emergency ward that night, would be observers of his work. The result was ramshackle as all hell but still looked deadly. Like I say, the gallows was the most interesting part of the whole scene. You could break your own neck if the stairs broke. They hauled him up there and gave him a flag to hold, behind his back. It looked a little like a funny tail the way he waved it around, so I turned to describe this scene to the mice, but they evidently had had enough and gone off to the kitchen to steal something to eat, their grades secure.

Can You Laugh Underwater?

If I didn't laugh then, why should I laugh now? My perception hasn't altered. I might be tired, laughter floating out of me unexpectedly like the child I always wanted. A child like a flying squirrel. A child that flies effortlessly and soundlessly. A child with flying squirrel eyes, that when I look into them there is a connection so water-deep it's physical, and I recoil as if I were staring down into light-less water with my snorkel. My great tail fins push me along through the empty water. No, I take that back. The water is full of luminescent jellyfish.

Reading at the Bowery Poet's Cafe

Where we are standing and sitting right now used to be underwater. Then not. Then, yes. Then, no. That was a nice nap. Everyone outside right now? Sleepwalkers. Take my advice and stay right here. Slaughterhouse five where we go to survive. Face it. This is wakefulness. One day all underwater again. Bring on the trilobites! They lasted for hundreds of millions of years, wrote poems predicting Ozymandias. That's real stone, baby. Real stone.

The Wind's Journey

The wind went south. It did not know why or what it would find there, or what psychological underpinnings motivated it, but it felt it might find something of an answer when it got there. After all, it isn't the journey that's important; the journey invariably sucks. It's the end that counts. After many adventures (see the seven volume *Stories of My Journey*), the wind came to a mountain far enough into the south where it was quickly and unfortunately enfolded in the hundred-thousand wings of monarch butterflies. This is the wrong place, it thought, I do not want to be where all this is already here. But where to go? For this there was no good or causally derivable answer.

Three-eyed Girl

Like Lem, I used to sneak into my father's surgery and look at what he had taken out of people's throats. When a little older, and bolder, I stole an unusually large black bean off the enameled tray out of the usual pile of stupid objects. I planted it in a small plastic pot and put it on my windowsill. Perhaps larks would come. That new moon, I was awakened suddenly by a three-eyed girl tapping on my cheek. She climbed into bed with me. I brushed the soil from her shoulders and we were married a short time later. My father, not a suspicious man, and not a little permissive with me ever since my mother had left with a bricklayer who lived nearby, never suspected a thing. We were always careful to pick the beans up off the floor of the bedroom after a new moon. We planted them in a field near the house, and began to raise an army to take over our little backward province, as a first step. After all, something had to be done, and if not by us, then who?

Some Pennies Are Rollers

I have four or five I keep in my pocket. One never knows when one might have to get out of certain situations, without the benefit of shoes, or other clothing.

Training

In my country, elephants run all the trains. Some other animals have applied for other jobs, but none do what elephants have accomplished. However, to be clear, all applications are carefully filed in an elegant, rather elaborate wooden trunk that is brought out once a year with great pomp and bunting. The elephants train it all over the country. People crowd up to the tracks to wave little flags with elephants on them, along with the glorious motto of our land: Only Water is Waterproof.

Thanks, God

They wore his and hers green fluorescent jackets, the same color as the vests workers along the roads wear nowadays. They often became disoriented otherwise, and tended to lose each other when they walked downtown. Now, and when they hold hands, they can glance sideways and be immediately reassured. Thank God for small but noticeable improvements.

Get to It

Old Peter used to limp around the lumber yard, yelling at us when we were kids to get away from this or get out of there or get to it. Down at the railroad station, different old men held tools or lanterns or waved towards one end of the train or the other. We ran along the tracks screaming like maniacs and then turned into the woods where the sun was dappled, green, and not so bright.

Inkadoo's Wings

Inkadoo had grown wings. They were large and abysmally tattered, partly since Inkadoo had been residing in a moldy alley tunneled with garbage tossed out of the apartment windows above. Did I tell you it was in this very city we are in right now, part mercantile, rotted from within? Even the sun seemed to regard the broken windows, fractured streets, and palsied souls as an enemy, worthy only of punishment. Nothing the sun disclosed was pleasant to any of the senses. A video news team was dispatched to cover this unbelievable event, Inkadoo's that is, but when he would not come out of the alley in daylight and only waved his wings listlessly, ineffectually, and in shadow, the producer nixed the video footage, using only a head-shot and an equally vague and short, unconvincing account by the reporter, ending with social services being called. Without the wings none of this would have been news of any kind. Here, look, I keep one of his feathers in this box. It is my dearest possession. Do you not agree?

The Birthday

I am reading Charles Simic. No surprise in that except he kept withdrawing his hand before proffering it again, over and over. As if, yes, this is my destiny, tell me, and then changing not his mind exactly but his mind's behavior. He would look at his hand each time and then lo! pick up the pencil or pen or crayon or stylus once more, and write (for example) about the silver dollar a magician had caused to fall out of his mouth on the magician's command to say the word *money*. Charles Simic's own twelve-year-old mouth! The magician winked at him, put a finger to his lips, and whispered, "Hold on to it. There's magic for you."

Trying to Get Eurydice to Answer the Phone

No matter how many pills you take out of the bottle, the lake at the bottom is still full of rocks. Listen to me, you idiot, how am I to get the shoelaces I want when you are constantly on the loose or rendered as a Babylonian mosaic because the pills have become mice with wings or parakeets with whiskers? This is not an idyl business you know, or should know, endlessly calling and calling my name into the darkness, trying to get Eurydice to answer the phone. There's too much sense and incense in this room. I can hardly breathe. Excuse me if I cause a few exotic birds to die with my exquisite eyelashes. Inexplicable fragility. Blink, blink.

A Letter

How did the little green frog become so hoarse? Stop it. Look how the iris makes its house. There is nothing for it. An oriole. Seashells. I apologize if I already mentioned this in my last letter. My voice was ruined after last night, and I caught a cold from the damp to boot. See you next Saturday, if nothing else collapses.

The Ritual

The coffin was tiny, made for a baby. All the candles skittering around it were embarrassed to be there, as was I, an innocent child, also slaughtered in the affair, but sewn up for the occasion, although my arms had been reversed and my fingers were sewn to my neck as if to say, when this is over, back you go. I don't know how they got all of Allan into that little case, considering he was ten years older than myself and tall, and not a little overweight. The next step in the ritual was to open the box and welcome Allan into the underworld by throwing tiny toy cars at him until the box was full. Then it was welded shut and auctioned off within two hours to the assembled priests waiting in the street outside. They would fight with whomever won the bid, sometimes killing the winner, and then the whole process would start over again.

After All

I am thrilled to receive this award, and so is someone to my left. Let us sing together of old days and fun ways, and then there will be time for everyone present to jump into the bottomless hole in the middle of the room. Except for me. After all, I am the award winner. Emphasis on 'after all.' This cake, made of green linnets and last kindnesses, I eat alone, in quiet, if not in peace.

True Sorrow

Whenever a bird sings, another hour is gone. Days pass by the window. Glancing in, the birds have smile wrinkles around their eyes, and I have yet to see my way clear to granting my cousin even a shoe. He needs the shoe so he can get to work. Other things have been mentioned but none that moved me to action or anything else describable. This moment of true sorrow is brought to you by a shoe.

Moon Dust

The way it turned out, the moon wasn't made out of cheese or cantaloupe. It was dust. "It looks better from here," Arnold said, throwing yet another stone into the surf.

Jellyfish

The green apple hung in the sky, glowing like a paper lantern. You know, in these intimate moments, your hand somewhere roaming my body, I always seem to return to the idea, if not the reality, of jellyfish. And if you could swish your hand around in my body as if it were a body of water, parts of me would suddenly glow. I am sure of it.

Gardening

Henry shouted across the room to Harriett. The room served as an ocean, a mountain, a large ugly rat, between their two raddled lives and the porch where they sometimes sat at night, in the summer, on the swing.

"Harriett!" shouted Henry, "I forgot the lightbulb."

"There will be another century. You can go then, when walking is once again fashionable!" Harriett yelled back, but with less anxiety, less grating desperation.

"Did you hear that?" muttered Arbaloc to his partner, Toraloc. "There they go again. They should really get outside more and garden the way we do. Sort of." And they, sighing, bent back to the earth where they were growing something that looked like plants, some with eyes, some with ears. All evidently juicy and delectable when cooked with both willing hands and hearts.

The Dream

The dream was not altogether disturbing, and it was "in color," but he awoke in a sweat not caused by the room. The fan wasn't on. That wasn't all: his feet seemed to have become transparent. None of it made any sense. He always slept in a two or three-foot pile of letters, his fan mail. He never took drugs. He did drink tea, but only because it tasted so good, especially Earl Grey, which made him think of how disgusting it would be if there really was anything of Earl Grey in it. His friend Earl, whose name happened to be also Earl Grey, assured him there was nothing to it. However, whenever Earl was over and they were having tea, he couldn't not look at Earl speculatively, wondering just what would that mean if there was something to it?

The Speaking Deep in the Forest

Down deep in the forest where lived the animals that spoke, there also lived a rock where the animals congregated. Although the animals talked to each other when they were at the rock and didn't try to eat others if they were predators, their hygienic habits were universally unchanged. The birds were the worst. The trees were mostly standoffish, whispering to each other overhead. The trees were waste eaters at ground level, meditators of sky and sun, moon and stars, wind, and ballooning spiders in their canopies. The rock was long-suffering, not given to conversation. Moody perhaps, sulky maybe, retired and laconically observational. And forever dirty with the droppings and washes of all kinds of creatures. People had long since died out and were forgotten. Occasionally, some artifact of human ingenuity and hubris would interfere with the workings of the world. Thus were the consequences of the human felt in a jarring and dissociative manner. As if the lightning had decided to start sporting a polka-dotted bow-tie, or the rock suddenly broke out yodeling. No, no. Animals that had been domesticated were wild or had not survived their freedom. None of this was remembered. The speaking deep in the forest around and on the rock mostly centered on what was invitational and unavoidable. This state of affairs went on until conversations became so sophisticated and nuanced that some animals fell into a state where they forgot to be animals. Not all of them came to a horrible end.

Clarity

Black espresso, clouded moonless unlit nights, my black mood under heavy trees at a table no one can see. I can feel the ink-sprayed fog descend into darkness. When no light comes from behind to illuminate, there is only this clarity, this empty self, waiting across from me.

Mission

There was a town where all the dogs had only three legs. No, wait a sec, that town outlawed dogs altogether. I saw one of these banished creatures loitering at the edge of the town limits under a sign that read Welcome to K____. The dog was clearly pining for its companion, a girl of about ten or so, who had been saddened for life because of the cruel ordinance foisted upon her by the town "fathers" and supported by her parents, who were secretly glad to see the animal gone. They dreamed of saving the dog-expense money to take a long-delayed honeymoon trip to Hawaii. Delayed being one form of the verb never. The mother did not enjoy or like her body as she once did. She no longer wanted to take her clothes off on a black obsidian beach where heavily inked Hawaiian men would dance wildly and masturbate until the ocean was a foaming frenzy. She now had other ideas, fuzzier plans. By now Hawaii was better in both their minds than it would ever be in reality. The dog, heartbroken and moaning, lay down under the sign. "I am so tired," it whispered. "Everything I ever desired is inside an invisible, forbidding fence. Ironic is it not?" And my mission, long sought for, was disclosed to me at last.

The Boat

Sometimes singly, or in pairs, occasionally in clusters, they came aboard the boat. The boat went away and was never seen again.

The Apprentice

My apprentice said to me yesterday, "Yesterday, as you asked me, I watched all the other masters at their work. The only thing I could see that was the same was that at the end, their pieces were all magnificent." "Yes, but what of their breath? And did you smell their feet before you kissed their hands?" "No." "So answer me this: why do you study under me and not one of them?" My apprentice thought for a moment, then replied; "What is the next thing you want me to do?" I turned away to smile. "Visit them once more, only this time …"

May I Sit in the Palm of Your Hand?

The whole band of us that you see here, we live in a hollow log. The fact that we are only six inches or so high is no bar to our reality. If we can, as has been rumored by others, fly, because of our unique relationship to gravity, that is either true or not. And as you are in some special sort of dream state, please remember that time still passes for us if not exactly in the same "frame" as for you. This is to correct the misapprehension that somehow the physical laws of the universe don't apply to us as they do to you. Interesting, don't you think, how dark it is and yet you can see everything. May I sit in the palm of your hand? We dressed up thinking you might come; it's Scottish style, tartans, wide belts, tams, though we dispensed with the shoes. No nettles here! Come, let's go into the log. Don't worry about proportions, somehow it all works, and we can all have tea. Do you care for crumpets? or pikelets? We feel that when the imagination is good food, inventiveness, wit, Hu Kwa, humor … you take my meaning.

Wet Dreams

When she told me she did sexual work for money, I was unprepared and pulled my hand from hers and stepped back, which was unfortunate because I fell backward off the stone embankment we were strolling along so comfortably and dropped into the river. Treacherous Paris! And I've never even been there! Oh Poe! Oh all right, Baudelaire! Oh oh oh! And now I am almost too old to travel and see the streets where Beckett would have walked, carrying his secret messages to undermine the forces of evil. Now my wet dreams are all about falling into the Seine! And finally I may have to suffer that ultimate insult of floating by the great fascist cathedral raised to the failure of being human. My sin!

The Hallway of Clocks

There! Take that! And my foot came down on the empty butter box, flattened it righteously and put it in the paper bag for recycling, along with the news, old music sheets and misprinted pages from the printer. What a great start to a short story, full of ambiguous energy, and contemporary. I looked over to my wife sitting in her rocker. Perhaps she was dozing, certainly she didn't hear my stomping. She's in her eighties and her wings have withered along with her hearing. I'm in my thirties, but we still love each other passionately and completely. So I gave up on the short story idea and instead helped her up so we could walk down the long, dark hallway of clocks to our bedroom.

Books

The books on the shelf were arguing, elbowing their neighbors like children unhappy with their place at table. I told them if they were so unhappy with where they were, they should speak to me about solutions, but they all intransigently clammed up. I heard one of them mutter, "He reads us, never asks us what we want, it's like slavery, don't say a word." And except for scolding them like kids lined up in a classroom for their naive fantasies about what they were and were not, there wasn't much I could do. Randomly move them around on the shelf, but was that really necessary? Were they just playing with my mind? I took one down, a beautiful hardcover edition of the *Philosophical Investigations*. Whodunit crime stories told in aphorisms. One of my favorites. Pretty clever. Actually more like genius. One can say that about the long dead. I stroked the cover, the binding, the tightly clasped pages. I do this before I ever start reading any of them, returning and reading as if for the first time. "I will keep you away from fire and I will keep you away from water," I whispered. My whole library. Ecstasy.

In the Darkest, Least-traveled Part of the Forest

Deep in the darkest, least-traveled part of the forest, a deer was howling. When the forester came upon it, she attempted to calm things down – the mocking jays, snickering chipmunks, usually standoffish hares thumping in a mocking rhythm to the deer's gasps. Finally, the forester was able to ask the deer what the problem was. The deer stopped howling abruptly. The woods became still. Archaic. Darker. The scent of dirt. The deer vanished silently even further into the woods. The forester put her ticket book back in her vest. She wouldn't make her quota today, she thought. But the deer might pick up its pain again.

Sorrow

There was a rush for the best positions on the window, as the frost began to form from the condensed sorrow of the night. "Pattern. Pattern," the frost muttered over and over to itself, "there must be a pattern here somewhere. All I'm finding are tiny imperfections."

Connections

I have two heads. I have not tried to hide one of them, the one that has always been asleep. Recently, however, my other head has been sighing and occasionally twitching its mouth as though it might awaken. This has troubled me, as you might imagine. I am thirty-five, well established in my career, considering marriage. There is a possibility. I have always dreamed of a partnership with another unconnected soul, completely separate from my own. Now I have so much anxiety I don't sleep well without a pill here and there. I wake up, my other head is grumbling and looking fretful. I am afraid. Afraid that some day, in the middle of the day I will nod off, the sun will shine caressingly on my other head's eyes, a pear-blossom-laden breeze will brush by his nose, and whisper like a sparrow into his ears, "Wake up! Wake up!" What then will become of me? What happens if it turns out I am already connected, in a special way, to another soul, a different person without my thoughts or feelings, or even experience, and yet sharing the most intimate functions (and dysfunctions!) of our body? Our one body?

The Horn of One Note

The birds whistled their morning challenges in the pre-dawn light. All over the city, crushed cans felt their emptiness increase. Near-musical notes fell on the sidewalks, on the streets, on porch steps, or like newspapers filled with shredded tunes and stale ephemera. Everything stepping into the same river over and over, as if one baptism required a never-ending succession of ever less effective dips. A cloud with some darkness to it gathered over the city, a cloud in the shape of a horn. The Horn of One Note. That is when the trees shading the sidewalks began to drop their leaves as if running away. And this was the morning of the eighth day …

Homemade Cloud Chamber

Dear T –

I am of the opinion you felt that by slipping away to that so-called celebration of life-madness in the fields and woods in the middle of our state that you would escape the mad-seeming influx of postcard after postcard from me. Inasmuch as you know me well enough and that your absence from your mailing address might curtail my efforts (my art, as it were), because I like my postcards to be received deliberately in serial order, not piling up higgledy-piggledy to be rummaged through all at once, you are right. I will wait until I am assured that you have returned from "the war" to resume my small task of redemption, salvation, enlightenment, or punishment, in whatever manner you so generously choose. I am embarking on a great postcard project, and you are one of the participants. I beg your indulgence, your good humor, your inquisitive laziness, as I begin this radiational experiment. You know, or should remember, those particles we observed with such perfect fascination in that homemade cloud chamber our father fashioned for us as children. The poet wrote, "Some say the world will end in fire, some say in ice." Well, between the dry ice and the alcohol, we watched the universe going about its eternal, ephemeral business-as-usual. The postcards are simply more of those particles trailing not so much a cloud, as a gesture of glory, to mis-paraphrase another poet. As Gertrude Stein might say, prepare for words, and then more words. Also the obligatory picture.

Your doting brother, K

The Pond at Machu Picchu

Morton S. spinning the music, spinning his tales. "This next piece had its origins, its unconscious conception if you will, when I was at Machu Picchu with some other musicians. I was left alone for a bit on a high terrace, the spacious, even vast panorama of tropical landscape below and sky above breathtaking. And it was a little hard to catch my breath. The oxygen, you know, it's all down there in the Amazon Basin. Just then, as I was not thinking about anything in particular except maybe Edna St. Vincent Millay. Maybe her daughter, with whom I had been breathlessly in love and had had a terribly clandestine affair because of our age difference. Machu Picchu. A breeze moved over the stones and grass. I could hear it as if in some sort of huge space, a whisper far off but caressing my face at the same moment. So this is what I hope you experience as well. And, by the way, the rumor that I have webbed feet is a fact. This did not prevent me from scaling the mountain paths to the ancient sacred Inca site. But what you are about to hear, this is my true element."

His fans turned to look at each other, green in the face almost the color of some frogs, all wishing they could see him disrobed so they could examine his body minutely for other mystical anomalies. They hopped away to their ponds and pads, dreaming of the music and turning on their radios as soon as they were sunk back in.

Mothfall

When the moths came, it was late at night. We had already heard about them from other towns down the coast. They beat feebly against the windows we had closed, the dust of their wings leaving little prints on the glass that looked sometimes like leaves, sometimes like hands. In the morning it was cloudy. The dust from the moths was about a foot deep everywhere. Technically the dust was composed of scales, vaguely iridescent, fractal, exotic feathers under the microscope. But it was scary too, as if some distant magic volcano had sent its own weather far and farther out, turning the sunsets a rainbow of colors, shifting like auroras, damping the wind and our voices as if something we couldn't see or account for was planning, preparing …

A Cat

Sleeping, stretched out, heavily furred in this iteration, in front of the refrigerator, perhaps because of the vent at the bottom but just as likely not, twitching a little every few moments, dreaming perhaps, although not the usual commentary I am familiar with about dogs chasing something either through the woods or across the lawn (two oceans about which more another time), because this cat is an indoor animal. If I imagined myself into her dreams if such they are, and not merely her brain activity, what would I be, how would I look to someone who operates as much by scent and touch and possibly less interested in my brain productions and so puzzled, and for how long? I am sitting on the washing machine during its spin cycle, to keep it from clattering its way across the floor, considering my cat, Opal this time, not trying to be smart about it in most senses except perhaps the most abstract, if that is indeed a sense in some sense. Ah, the chemistry of dreaming and waking, how different they are whether we wish it or no. I look out the kitchen window at the morning glories on the back porch, blooming today dark purple even after noon because it is late summer but also maybe in part because it is a rainy day, less than 70° Fahrenheit. They seem to be declaring, trumpeting, calling forth, their shape helps define the words I am looking for for them. The dream of my cat, the silent yearning of the morning glories, somehow beyond the desire for offspring, somehow just themselves for a moment in some world we call our own, I am thrust by the forces of nature into some pause; no breeze, the cat still and relaxed, the washing machine done with wringing out what water was loose in its container. The dial has moved to "off."

Visit from God

God was despondent. I found the creature sitting disconsolately on my back porch steps (red bricks cemented over gray cinder blocks). At first I thought God was bouncing a ball off the driveway at his feet and catching it as it rose up, to a hand that seemed as human as yours or mine, then with a snap of the wrist sending it back down. My mistake. Or God's, it's a little hard to tell in these conditions. Normal daytime, calendrically correct in our ultimately entropic time frame, some sort of neutral bluish sky, sunny most of the time, green of the yard in my case (I don't live in an urban center) weather. Or was there an hallucinatory quality that made it epistemologically difficult to do anything other than report, subjective as that may seem. That's better. Just say it and be done with it. A friend had sent me a disc of Bach's Motets. I was playing them loud, loud enough to perturb the large koi in the upper pool where I had sunk a plastic trash can to offer it protection from osprey. Which by the way it didn't need anymore once the duckweed and the waterlily had grown in, and probably didn't need before that because I had strung some white string across the pool, to confuse or discourage any diving predators early on. "Why are you looking despondent?" I asked God. You can do this when God chooses to be in human form, and if you're around at the time. "Filling in a possibility," God said, and I was sorry I had missed the happy filling moment, but then we are stuck in a way that God isn't. We take what we get. Of course God is both stuck and not stuck at all, that's a big difference, or at least for a moment it seemed so, until God suddenly, and I mean Suddenly, instantly, like the space between one thought and the next, disappeared, leaving me standing there, free and clear, so to speak.

In This Next Breath

In this next breath, he wrote the fatal word Finis. Fine. End. The End: an end, the completion of the task even if not completed. There was the front and the back, dorsal ventral, hardback softcover, the thin page and the fingers behaving just in the right way, roiling in his mind to turn the last page. Temporary, of course. Time to slough that skin and get a move on. Return to waiting. So much to do while waiting! But to get there, in that fulfilling, aesthetic sense, he lived for that. His hands shook and not from any emotion, unless the body itself counted as an emotion. Some disconnected thoughts rustled their way through the dead leaves, sensing their separate (sort of) lives. Their close gray fur and quick heart. He loved them even if all he could do was observe them as they appeared suddenly and without expectation and then vanished along the track they had worn into the weeds and soil. The same grass and dirt that would erase them soon enough. Soon enough. There was the satisfying end that only art could or can provide (Provide! Provide!), the body being a vessel full of promise and empty of meaning.

Eric H. Edwards

Born in the Chenango Valley, New York, 1947.
Raised in Falmouth on Cape Cod (Woods Hole Village).
Schooled variously (Colgate University, Boston University).
Lives in Falmouth, Mass.
Tends Friends (Quakers), Flowers, Words.

www.ingramcontent.com/pod-product-compliance
Lightning Source LLC
Chambersburg PA
CBHW052205090526
44583CB00015BA/1574